Collins easy learning

French
Idioms

J'ai l'estomac
dans les talons!

Une histoire tirée
par les cheveux.

HarperCollins Publishers
Westerhill Road
Bishopbriggs
Glasgow
G64 2QT
Great Britain

First Edition 2010

Reprint 10 9 8 7 6 5

© HarperCollins Publishers 2010

Collins® is a registered trademark of
HarperCollins Publishers Limited

www.collinslanguage.com

A catalogue record for this book is
available from the British Library

ISBN 978-0-00-733735-4

Designed and typeset by Thomas Callan

Printed in Great Britain by
Clays Ltd, St Ives plc

Acknowledgements
We would like to thank those authors
and publishers who kindly gave
permission for copyright material
to be used in the Collins Word Web.
We would also like to thank Times
Newspapers Ltd for providing valuable
data.

PUBLISHING DIRECTOR
Rob Scriven

MANAGING EDITOR
Gaëlle Amiot-Cadey

PROJECT MANAGEMENT
Susie Beattie
Ben Harris

CONTRIBUTORS
Sabine Citron
Daphne Day
Laurent Jouet
Laurence Larroche

ILLUSTRATION AND IMAGE RESEARCH
Q2AMedia

William Collins' dream of knowledge for all began with the publication of his first book in 1819. A self-educated mill worker, he not only enriched millions of lives, but also founded a flourishing publishing house. Today, staying true to this spirit, Collins books are packed with inspiration, innovation, and practical expertise. They place you at the centre of a world of possibility and give you exactly what you need to explore it.

Language is the key to this exploration, and at the heart of Collins Dictionaries is language as it is really used. New words, phrases, and meanings spring up every day, and all of them are captured and analysed by the Collins Word Web. Constantly updated, and with over 2.5 billion entries, this living language resource is unique to our dictionaries. Words are tools for life. And a Collins Dictionary makes them work for you.

Collins. Do more.

Introduction

What is it?

Collins Easy Learning French Idioms is an invaluable resource for learners
of French who want to be able to communicate more naturally. It
will enable you to start to include colourful idiomatic phrases and
expressions in both your writing and conversation, increasing your
confidence and effectiveness. It can be used to develop your language
skills, whether you are studying French at school or university, at home
or at an evening class.

Why do you need it?

Developing expertise in writing, speaking and understanding a foreign
language means being able to pull together and build on a number of
different aspects – vocabulary, grammar, pronunciation, and so on. An
important element of increased proficiency in communication is the use
of idioms and figurative expressions which will add colour and variety
to your writing and conversation as well as enabling you to sound more
natural and confident. Idioms are phrases whose meaning may not be
obvious from the words they contain. For example, a common English
idiom is 'Add fuel to the fire'. If somebody adds fuel to the fire, they
make a bad situation worse.

How is it structured?

Collins Easy Learning French Idioms has been carefully designed to provide
a rich and easy-to-use resource for extending your language skills. It

contains 250 phrases and expressions, all of which have been selected because they are commonly used by French speakers today. These idioms are then arranged by theme, 25 in all. Each of these subjects covers an area of everyday life or experience, such as 'Health, happiness, pleasure and enjoyment', 'Madness, foolishness and stupidity', and 'Directness, decisiveness and expressing opinions'.

For maximum clarity, each French idiom is followed by a word-for-word English translation as well as the equivalent idiomatic expression(s) that you would use in English. In many cases, a short background note is included if some explanation or additional information about French language or culture is required. Then, in order to illustrate the use of the idiom in a natural context, a sentence or two of French is provided. Again, this is translated into idiomatic English. For example:

avoir le cafard (informal)

> *"to have the cockroach"*
> = to have the blues
> = to be feeling down

● Another expression for this is avoir le
   bourdon, literally *to have the bumblebee*.

**Si vous avez le cafard, ne restez pas seul :
rien de tel qu'une sortie entre amis
pour vous changer les idées et oublier
vos problèmes.**

If you're feeling down, don't stay on
your own: there is nothing like going
out with your friends to take your
mind off things and help you forget your problems.

Why choose Collins Easy Learning French Idioms?

- **easy to use**: 250 colourful idiomatic expressions arranged in 25 themes to do with daily life and common experience
- **easy to read**: a clear, modern layout which allows you to find the information you want quickly and easily
- **easy to understand**: written in an accessible style with the language you will hear from French speakers today

The Collins Easy Learning range

The Collins Easy Learning French Idioms is the latest addition to the bestselling Collins Easy Learning range, which includes the highly acclaimed Collins Easy Learning French Dictionary. Collins Easy Learning French Grammar and Collins Easy Learning French Verbs support you with all your grammatical needs, while the Collins Easy Learning French Words and Collins Easy Learning French Conversation allow you to learn and practise your French vocabulary and communication skills. The Collins Easy Learning series is the ideal language reference range to help you learn French.

Contents

Contents

Hope, dreams, fear and anxiety

Anger, annoyance, threats and violence

Truth, honesty, lying and deceit

Contents

Love, affection, marriage and friendship

Argument, conflict, help and cooperation

Telling off, praise, critics and criticism

Mistakes, shame and embarrassment

Knowledge, intelligence, ignorance and understanding

Contents

Looks, appearance, beauty and vanity

Madness, foolishness and stupidity

Relationships, similarities and differences

Problems, difficulties, the possible and the impossible

Orders, obedience, control and equality

Work, laziness, effort and ambition

Change, continuity, risk and opportunity

Contents

Eating, drinking, drunkenness and excess

Directness, decisiveness and expressing opinions

Money, debt, wealth and poverty

Language, speech, silence and conversation

Contents

Youth, experience, age and death

Easy Learning
French
Idioms

Health, happiness,
pleasure and enjoyment

être aux anges

> "to be with the angels"
> = to be in seventh heaven

● The exact equivalent of the English, *to be in seventh heaven* also exists in French, être au septième ciel.

Emmanuelle était aux anges quand on lui a appris qu'elle venait de gagner un safari en Afrique.
Emmanuelle was in seventh heaven when she heard that she had won a safari in Africa.

reprendre du poil de la bête (informal)

"to have more of the hair of the beast"
= to be on the mend again

The meaning of the English expression *hair of the dog* only relates to alcohol: the French is a more positive expression; it comes from the belief that if you apply the hair of the beast that bit you to your wound, you will feel better.

Hélène est sortie de l'hôpital il y a quelques jours seulement, mais à la grande surprise de tous les médecins, elle a déjà repris du poil de la bête.
Hélène only came out of hospital a few days ago but to the great surprise of all the doctors she is already on the mend again.

sabler le champagne

"to drink the champagne in one go"
= to crack open the champagne

Les résultats officiels du vote n'ont pas encore été annoncés, mais au siège du parti on se prépare déjà à sabler le champagne.
The official results of the vote have not yet been announced but at party headquarters they are already preparing to crack open the champagne.

se porter comme un charme

> *"to feel like a charm"*
> = to be as fit as a fiddle

● Also **aller comme un charme**. A healthy glow sometimes involves a bit of magic!

– **Tiens, j'ai croisé David au marché ce matin, et il m'a demandé de tes nouvelles.**
– **Ah ? Et comment va-t-il ?**
– **Il se porte comme un charme.**
"Hey, I ran into David at the market this morning, and he asked after you."
"Oh? And how is he?"
"He's as fit as a fiddle."

de derrière les fagots *(informal)*

> *"from behind the firewood"*
> = extra-special

● The idea here is that the oldest (and best) wine was stored in the back of the cellar, behind the piles of firewood.

Ce soir dans notre émission, une programmation musicale de derrière les fagots, concoctée spécialement pour vous par notre célèbre animateur, DJ Rich !
This evening we're broadcasting an extra-special programme of music devised specially for you by our famous presenter, DJ Rich!

pas piqué des hannetons (*informal*)

> *"not eaten by cockchafers"*
> = brilliant

● Also pas piqué des vers, literally *not eaten by worms.*

Quand sa voiture toute neuve est tombée en panne pour la troisième fois en un mois, Patrick a écrit à son concessionnaire pour se plaindre. J'ai lu la lettre : elle **était pas piquée des hannetons** !
When his brand new car broke down for the third time in a month, Patrick wrote to his dealer to complain. I've read the letter: it's brilliant!

faire la grasse matinée

> *"to make a fat morning"*
> = to have a lie-in

Pendant la semaine on se lève à 6h00 tous les jours, donc en général on profite du dimanche pour **faire la grasse matinée**.
During the week we get up at 6am every day so we generally make sure we have a lie-in on Sundays.

être à l'aise dans ses baskets (informal)

"to be fine in your trainers"
= to be comfortable with yourself
= to be at ease with yourself

Also **être bien dans ses baskets.**

Yohann, vingt ans, à l'aise dans ses baskets avec son sourire irrésistible et une brillante carrière d'architecte devant lui.
Yohann is a 20-year-old who's very much at ease with himself. He has an irresistible smile and a glittering career as an architect ahead of him.

être aux petits oignons (informal)

"to be cooked with pickling onions"

= to be perfect

A dish cooked with small onions is said to be a perfect dish. You can also find the expression **soigner quelqu'un aux petits oignons** (to treat somebody like a king (or queen)).

En Formule 1, les mécaniciens travaillent souvent des nuits entières pour que la voiture soit aux petits oignons.
In Formula One, the mechanics often work through the night to make sure the car is perfect.

Unhappiness, sickness, grief and disappointment

avoir le cafard (informal)

"to have the cockroach"
= to have the blues
= to be feeling down

Another expression for this is **avoir le bourdon**, literally *to have the bumblebee*.

Si vous **avez le cafard,** ne restez pas seul : rien de tel qu'une sortie entre amis pour vous changer les idées et oublier vos problèmes.
If you're feeling down, don't stay on your own: there is nothing like going out with your friends to take your mind off things and help you forget your problems.

filer un mauvais coton

"to spin a bad thread"
= to be in a bad way
= to be going downhill

● As well as the physical sense, this expression can have a moral sense, *to get into bad ways.*

Les trois derniers films de ce réalisateur ont reçu un accueil mitigé, et même chez ses plus fervents admirateurs, on dit qu'il file un mauvais coton.
This director's last three films have received a mixed reception, and even his most passionate admirers are saying he's going downhill.

la goutte d'eau qui fait déborder le vase

"the drop of water that makes the vase overflow"
= the last straw
= the straw that broke the camel's back

● This expression also exists in Spanish and Italian.

Pour les habitants du quartier excédés par les incivilités quotidiennes, cette agression est la goutte d'eau qui a fait déborder le vase : ils ont organisé une manifestation devant la mairie.
For the people living in the neighbourhood, who are infuriated by daily incidents of anti-social behaviour, this attack is the last straw: they have organised a demonstration in front of the town hall.

pleurer comme une Madeleine

"to cry like Mary Magdalene"

= to cry your eyes out

● This phrase refers to the grief shown by Mary Magdalene at the crucifixion of Jesus.

Elle pleure comme une Madeleine depuis deux jours parce que son chat ne revient pas.
She's been crying her eyes out for two days because her cat has not come back.

la montagne accouche d'une souris

> "the mountain gives birth to a mouse"
> = great expectations come to nothing

Après des mois de négociations et un sommet international pour mettre fin au conflit, la montagne accouche d'une souris : aucun accord de paix n'a été signé.

After months of negotiations and an international summit to end the conflict, great expectations come to nothing: no peace deal has been signed.

avoir du plomb dans l'aile

> "to have lead in the wing"
> = to be in a bad way

Suite aux récentes révélations concernant sa vie privée, la carrière du présentateur a du plomb dans l'aile.

Following recent revelations concerning his private life, the presenter's career is in a bad way.

tomber dans les pommes (informal)

> "to fall in the apples"
> = to faint
> = to pass out

Au dernier réveillon, Sébastien s'est coupé en ouvrant les huîtres ; il est immédiatement tombé dans les pommes car il ne supporte pas la vue du sang.
Last New Year's Eve, Sébastien cut himself opening oysters; he immediately passed out because he can't stand the sight of blood.

manger de la vache enragée

"to eat rabid cow"
= to go through hard times
= to have a very hard time of it

This means you're so poor you're forced to eat meat which has come from a cow with rabies.

C'était un artiste révolté qui, avant d'être reconnu pour son travail, **a mangé de la vache enragée** pendant des années.
He was a rebellious artist who had a very hard time of it for some years, before his work gained recognition.

ne pas en mener large

"not to do something in a big way"
= to feel small
= to be scared silly

Quand on est dans l'avion, sur le point de sauter en parachute, on **n'en mène pas large**.
When you are in an aeroplane, about to do a parachute jump, you're scared silly.

Achievement, success, failure and misfortune

arriver dans un fauteuil (informal)

"to arrive in an armchair"

= to romp home

●   The idea here is that arriving somewhere in an armchair has meant you have had to exert no effort at all.

Le maire, qui se présentait pour un troisième mandat, a été réélu dans un fauteuil malgré la présence de cinq autres candidats.

The mayor, who put himself up for a third term, has romped home despite the presence of five other candidates.

bien mener sa barque

>"*to steer one's boat well*"
>= to do alright for yourself

● But be careful: **charger sa barque** means *to overdo it*.

Personne ne s'attendait à ce qu'elle réussisse, mais elle a bien mené sa barque et occupe maintenant un poste prestigieux.
Nobody expected her to succeed but she did alright for herself and now holds a prestigious post.

les carottes sont cuites *(informal)*

>"*the carrots are cooked*"
>= it's all over

● For the French it's the humble carrot that gets cooked – not the goose.

Et un troisième but marqué par l'Italie à quelques minutes de la fin du match ! On peut maintenant dire que pour l'équipe de France, les carottes sont cuites.
And a third goal scored by Italy a few minutes from the end of the game! We can now say it's all over for the French team.

faire chou blanc *(informal)*

> *"to make white cabbage"*
> = to draw a blank

● By contrast, faire ses choux gras de quelque chose means *to make the most of something.*

Braquage de la bijouterie : l'enquête fait chou blanc, la police relâche le suspect principal.
Robbery at jeweller's: the investigation draws a blank, police release the prime suspect.

être au creux de la vague

> *"to be in the trough of the wave"*
> = to have hit rock bottom
> = to be at the lowest ebb

Pour un secteur du tourisme qui est déjà au creux de la vague, cet été pluvieux est une catastrophe.
For a tourist industry which has already hit rock bottom, this wet summer is a disaster.

tirer son épingle du jeu

"to pull one's pin from the game"
= to extricate yourself from a tricky situation
= to emerge unscathed

This expression seems to refer to a traditional game in which the aim was to get your own pin back out of a heap.

La compétition est rude, mais pour ceux qui réussissent à tirer leur épingle du jeu, les perspectives sont intéressantes.
The competition is tough but for those who manage to emerge unscathed, the prospects are good.

faire contre mauvaise fortune bon cœur

"to show courage in the face of bad luck"
= to make the best of it

Here, **cœur** means *courage* rather than *heart*.

Je voulais du sorbet à la pêche mais il n'en restait plus, alors j'ai fait contre mauvaise fortune bon cœur et j'ai pris la crème brûlée.
I wanted peach sorbet but there wasn't any left so I made the best of it and had the crème brûlée.

donner sa langue au chat

"to give your tongue to the cat"
= to give up

This expression means *to give your tongue to the cat* because it's of no use to you, since you don't have the answers.

Ses devinettes sont trop difficiles : nous finissons toujours par donner notre langue au chat.
His riddles are too difficult: we always give up in the end.

se faire rouler dans la farine (informal)

> "to be rolled in the flour"
> = to be had

The French rouler quelqu'un dans la farine means *to dupe somebody*.

Pour acheter sur internet sans se faire rouler dans la farine, il faut prendre un certain nombre de précautions.
To buy online without being had, you need to take a number of precautions.

passer comme une lettre à la poste (informal)

> "to go like a letter into the letterbox"
> = to go off without a hitch
> = to work perfectly

The idea here is that a letter slides easily into a letterbox.

L'excuse qu'il a donnée pour expliquer son absence était invraisemblable, mais elle est passée comme une lettre à la poste.
The excuse he gave to explain his absence was unbelievable but it worked perfectly.

tirer les marrons du feu

"to pull the chestnuts out of the fire"
= to do the dirty work

Ils vont en profiter alors que nous avons pris tous les risques :
encore une fois c'est nous qui allons **tirer les marrons du feu.**
They are going to get the benefit when we took all the risks: once
again we're the ones who'll do the dirty work.

faire d'une pierre deux coups

"to make two hits with one stone"
= to kill two birds with one stone

En augmentant le prix des cigarettes, le gouvernement **fait d'une pierre deux coups** : il renforce sa lutte anti-tabac et augmente ses recettes.
By increasing the price of cigarettes, the government is killing two birds with one stone: it strengthens its anti-smoking campaign and increases its revenue.

tuer la poule aux œufs d'or

"to kill the hen with the golden eggs"
= to kill the goose that lays the golden egg

En développant le tourisme dans les parcs naturels, on risque de **tuer la poule aux œufs d'or,** car les visites permettent de financer des projets, mais elles occasionnent bien souvent des dégâts environnementaux irréversibles.
By developing tourism in nature reserves there is a risk of killing the goose that lays the golden egg, since visitors bring in money that helps finance projects, but very often bring about irreversible environmental damage.

faire un tabac (informal)

> *"to make a noise"*
> = to be a big hit
> = to be a roaring success

tabac can mean *tobacco*, but is also slang for a hit or success.

Le film, qui **a fait un tabac** en France avec plus de cinq millions d'entrées, vient d'être nominé aux Oscars.
The film, which was a big hit in France with more than five million tickets sold, has been nominated for the Oscars.

Hope, dreams, fear and anxiety

se faire un sang d'encre

> *"to turn your blood to ink"*
> = to be worried sick

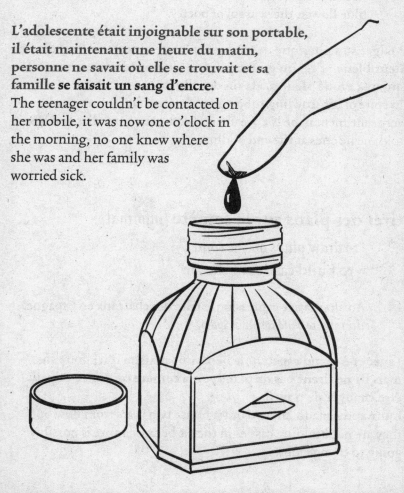

Also **se faire des cheveux blancs**, literally *to make your hair white*.

L'adolescente était injoignable sur son portable, il était maintenant une heure du matin, personne ne savait où elle se trouvait et sa famille se faisait un sang d'encre.
The teenager couldn't be contacted on her mobile, it was now one o'clock in the morning, no one knew where she was and her family was worried sick.

être fleur bleue *(informal)*

"to be a blue flower"
= to be naïvely sentimental

This expression originates in a story by the young German Romantic, Novalis, about a wandering minstrel who finds a blue flower, the symbol of poetry.

Malgré son physique de rugbyman renfrogné, Jean-Paul est très fleur bleue : c'est un grand amateur de comédies sentimentales qui m'a avoué pleurer à la fin des films.
In spite of his scowling rugby player's appearance, Jean-Paul is very sentimental: he is a great fan of romantic comedies and has told me he cries at the end of films.

tirer des plans sur la comète *(informal)*

"to draw plans on the comet"
= to build castles in the air

An alternative expression is **faire des châteaux en Espagne**, literally *to build castles in Spain*.

Laure et Arnaud espèrent acheter une maison d'ici deux ans, mais ils ne tirent pas de plans sur la comète car Laure va peut-être changer de travail.
Laure and Arnaud hope to buy a house two years from now but they are not building castles in the air because Laure is possibly going to change jobs.

avoir les jetons (informal)

> "to have the chips"
> = to be petrified
> = to have the jitters

If you placed your chips (**jetons**) at the roulette table, you would probably also be scared of losing them.

Pour rentrer à la maison il fallait passer devant le cimetière. La nuit, on avait les jetons, alors on se mettait à courir.
To get home we had to go past the cemetery. At night, we were petrified so we used to run all the way.

promettre monts et merveilles

> "to promise mountains and marvels"
> = to promise the earth

Pendant la campagne électorale, les candidats promettent monts et merveilles, mais une fois élus, ils reviennent vite à la réalité.
During the election campaign the candidates promise the earth but once elected, they quickly return to reality.

dormir sur ses deux oreilles

"to sleep on both your ears"
= to sleep soundly

Avec deux chiens de garde, une alarme et des caméras de vidéosurveillance partout dans son magasin, Michel peut **dormir sur ses deux oreilles**.
With two guard dogs, an alarm and CCTV cameras throughout his shop, Michel can sleep soundly.

c'est le cadet de mes soucis

"it's the youngest of my worries"
= that's the least of my worries

Il dérange tout le quartier avec sa musique, mais **c'est le cadet de ses soucis**.
He disturbs the whole neighbourhood with his music, but that's the least of his worries.

être dans la lune

"to be in the moon"
= to have one's head in the clouds
= to be in a dream

The moon is traditionally associated with dreams and otherworldliness.

C'était un élève discret en classe qui dessinait, écrivait des poèmes ou était tout simplement dans la lune.
He was an unobtrusive pupil at school who drew, wrote poems or was quite simply in a dream.

Anger, annoyance, threats and violence

la moutarde lui montait au nez

> *"the mustard got up his nose"*
> = he flared up
> = he saw red

La moutarde me monte au nez quand je vois des personnes valides garer leur voiture sur les places pour handicapés.
I see red when I come across able-bodied people parking their cars in accessible parking spaces.

défendre quelque chose bec et ongles

> *"to defend something with beak and claws"*
> = to fight tooth and nail for something

● A Latin version of **bec et ongles** is the motto of the historic city of Valence in southeastern France.

Elle a défendu bec et ongles le projet de théâtre sur lequel elle travaille depuis cinq ans.
She has fought tooth and nail for the theatre project which she has been working on for the last five years.

avoir le couteau sous la gorge

> *"to have the knife under the throat"*
> = to have a gun to the head

● If you are the aggressor, the expression is **mettre le couteau sous la gorge à quelqu'un** (*to put a gun to somebody's head*).

L'entreprise a le couteau sous la gorge : elle est très endettée, ses produits se vendent mal, elle doit accepter le partenariat pour ne pas faire faillite.
The company has a gun to its head: it is heavily in debt, its products are not selling: it must accept the partnership if it is not to go bankrupt.

quel navet ! (informal)

"what a turnip!"

= what a load of rubbish!

On lui offrait peu de rôles intéressants à l'époque alors, comme beaucoup d'autres acteurs, pour continuer à vivre de son métier il a joué dans des navets.

He was offered few interesting parts at the time so, like many other actors, to continue to make a living out of his profession he worked on some rubbishy films.

prendre la mouche

"to take the fly"
= to go into a huff
= to get huffy

The image here seems to be of an animal being bitten by a fly and sent mad by it.

Quand je lui ai fait remarquer que son bureau était en désordre, elle **a pris la mouche** et elle est sortie en claquant la porte.
When I pointed out to her that her desk was in a mess, she went into a huff and left the room, slamming the door behind her.

avoir un œil au beurre noir (informal)

"to have an eye in brown butter sauce"
= to have a black eye

Stéphanie ne s'est pas rendu compte que son fils était brutalisé à l'école jusqu'au jour où il est revenu à la maison avec **un œil au beurre noir**.
Stephanie did not realize that her son was being bullied at school until the day he came home with a black eye.

tirer sur l'ambulance

> *"to shoot at the ambulance"*
> = to kick someone when they are down

● This expression was coined by the French political journalist and one-time government minister, Françoise Giroud (1916-2003).

Ceux qui critiquent les organisations humanitaires tirent sur l'ambulance : elles manquent de moyens et doivent travailler dans des conditions dangereuses, souvent sans l'aide des grands pays.

Those who criticize humanitarian organisations are kicking them when they're down: they don't have enough resources and have to work in dangerous conditions, often without support from powerful nations.

s'attirer les foudres de quelqu'un

> *"to attract thunderbolts from somebody"*
> = to provoke an angry response from somebody

● Thunder and lightning were traditionally believed to be expressions of divine displeasure.

L'actrice s'est attiré les foudres du Vatican en critiquant le Pape.
The actress provoked an angry response from the Vatican by criticizing the Pope.

sortir de ses gonds

> *"to come off your hinges"*
> = to go berserk

● To make somebody wild with rage is **jeter quelqu'un hors de ses gonds**, literally *to throw somebody off their hinges*.

Quand l'assureur lui a appris qu'elle devrait payer les réparations, elle est sortie de ses gonds.
When the insurance company told her that she would have to pay for the repairs, she went berserk.

être soupe au lait

"to be milk soup"
= to have a short fuse

Watch how milk suddenly rises up when it comes to the boil and you have the graphic image behind this expression.

Notre professeur de français était très soupe au lait : au moindre bruit, il devenait tout rouge et entrait dans des colères terrifiantes.
Our French teacher had a very short fuse: at the slightest sound he would go bright red and fly into a terrifying rage.

Truth, honesty, lying and deceit

se mettre le doigt dans l'œil

"to put your finger in your eye"
= to be kidding yourself

A more informal way of saying this in French would be **se fourrer le doigt dans l'œil**, literally *to stuff your finger in your eye*.

Ceux qui croient aux promesses de la direction se mettent le doigt dans l'œil : il n'y aura pas d'augmentation !
People who believe the promises made by management are kidding themselves: there won't be a pay rise!

jouer l'arlésienne

"to play the girl from Arles"
= to fail to materialize

This expression originates from a tragic story by Alphonse Daudet, set to music by Bizet, in which a girl from Arles is awaited by her lover but never appears.

Le projet de troisième aéroport à Paris joue l'arlésienne depuis près de quarante ans. Personne ne sait s'il verra le jour.
The project for a third airport in Paris has failed to materialize for nearly 40 years. No one knows if it will see the light of day.

mener en bateau

"to take away by boat"
= to take for a ride
= to lead up the garden path

Quand ils arrivent enfin à destination, les voyageurs se rendent compte qu'on les a menés en bateau : l'hôtel est sale et délabré, le guide ne parle pas un mot de français et le programme des visites n'est pas respecté.
When they finally arrive at their destination, the travellers realize that they have been taken for a ride: the hotel is dirty and dilapidated, the guide speaks not a word of French and the tour programme is ignored.

pas très catholique *(informal)*

> *"not very catholic"*
> = a bit dodgy

● Expressions connected with Roman Catholicism are common in countries like France with a strong religious history. Interestingly, an equivalent expression in English would be *not kosher*.

Ma compagne a été malade toute la nuit. Il faut dire que le restaurant où l'on a mangé n'était pas très catholique.
My partner has been ill all night. To be honest, the restaurant we ate at was a bit dodgy.

une histoire à dormir debout

> *"a story to make you sleep standing up"*
> = a cock-and-bull story

● Some animals may be able to do it, but humans don't generally sleep standing up. Hence this expression.

Il m'a raconté comment il est arrivé en France à l'âge de quatorze ans dans le coffre d'une voiture : c'est une histoire à dormir debout !
He told me how he arrived in France at the age of 14 in the boot of a car: a cock-and-bull story!

faire l'école buissonnière

> *"to make school in the bush"*
> = to play truant

● The idea here seems to be that hiding in the bushes is as good a way as any of avoiding school.

Beaucoup d'élèves font l'école buissonnière et passent leurs journées dans les centres commerciaux alors que leurs parents les croient en classe.
Many pupils play truant and spend their days in shopping centres when their parents think they are at school.

c'est cousu de fil blanc

> *"it's stitched with white thread"*
> = it's blatant
> = it's perfectly predictable

● The idea here is that white tacking or stitching thread in a coloured garment is highly visible and undesirable.

La sentence du tribunal contre l'opposant n'a surpris personne : le procès était cousu de fil blanc.
The court's sentencing of the defendant surprised no one: the outcome of the trial was perfectly predictable.

montrer patte blanche

> *"to show a white paw"*
> = to show your credentials

This expression was made popular by the fable about a wolf, a goat and its kid. Left at home alone, the kid was told only to open the door to an animal that could show a white paw. The wolf, having grey paws, was thus kept at bay.

**Pour entrer dans le bâtiment, il faut montrer patte blanche :
chaque employé doit présenter sa carte à l'entrée et connaître le
code de son service.**
To gain entrance to the building you have to show
your credentials: each employee has to present
their card at the entrance and know their
department code.

vendre la mèche

"to sell the fuse"
= to give the game away
= to let the cat out of the bag

If the fuse of a bomb is discovered in time, the bomb can be defused. So the fuse represents something which shouldn't be revealed.

La veille du jour où le braquage était prévu, la police vient frapper à sa porte pour l'arrêter : l'un de ses complices, pris de panique, a vendu la mèche.
The day before the robbery was to take place, the police came to his door to arrest him: one of his accomplices panicked and gave the game away.

mettre quelqu'un au pied du mur

"to put somebody at the foot of the wall"
= to get somebody up against a wall

If you get somebody up against a wall, they are trapped and cannot escape.

Les manifestants ont mis le gouvernement au pied du mur : des négociations doivent débuter la semaine prochaine.
The protesters have got the government up against a wall. So much so, that negotiations are due to start next week.

découvrir le pot aux roses (informal)

> "to discover the pot of roses"
> = to discover the truth accidentally
> = to find out what's been going on

Elle a découvert le pot aux roses en tombant sur un SMS envoyé à son mari par sa maîtresse.
She discovered the truth when she came across a text to her husband from his mistress.

au nez et à la barbe de quelqu'un

"under somebody's nose and beard"
= under somebody's nose

**Après la défaite de ses troupes, il fuit le pays au nez et à la barbe
de l'ennemi en se déguisant en femme.**
After the defeat of his troops, he fled the country under the
enemy's nose by disguising himself as a woman.

remettre les pendules à l'heure (informal)

"to reset the clocks to the right time"
= to set the record straight

**Pour mettre fin aux tensions, la directrice a remis les pendules
à l'heure lors d'une réunion avec les chefs de service.**
To put an end to the tensions, the director set the record straight
at a meeting with department heads.

deux poids deux mesures

> *"two weights two measures"*
> = double standards

Après le verdict, les avocats ont déclaré que la peine très sévère prononcée contre leur client prouve qu'il y a **deux poids deux mesures**.

After the verdict, the lawyers declared that the very harsh penalty handed down to their client is proof of double standards.

raconter des salades *(informal)*

> *"to tell salads"*
> = to spin yarns
> = to tell stories

Just as salads are mixtures of different types of leaf, so the stories we tell can be mixtures of truth and fabrication.

Arrête de **raconter des salades** ! On t'a vu avec cette femme, on a même des photos de vous deux ensemble !

Stop telling stories! You've been seen with that woman, there are even photos of the two of you together!

se mettre à table (informal)

"to sit at the table"

= to come clean

Voilà bientôt six heures que les deux enquêteurs interrogent le suspect pour obtenir des aveux, mais sans résultat : il refuse de **se mettre à table.**

The two investigators have been questioning the suspect for almost six hours, in hopes of getting a confession, but with no success: he refuses to come clean.

prendre des vessies pour des lanternes (informal)

"to mistake bladders for lanterns"

= to have the wool pulled over your eyes

= to be taken in

Inflated pigs' bladders were sometimes used to hold candles and hung up as safety lamps.

Attention à ne pas **prendre des vessies pour des lanternes :** contrairement à ce que laisse entendre la publicité, il s'agit d'un yaourt et non d'un médicament.

Don't be taken in: contrary to what the adverts would have us believe, it's a yoghurt and not medicine.

Love, affection, marriage and friendship

avoir un cœur d'artichaut

> *"to have an artichoke heart"*
> = to fall in love with everyone you meet

● The idea here is that by the time you have reached the centre of the vegetable you have pulled off enough leaves to give one to everybody.

Celles et ceux qui ont un cœur d'artichaut ont une vie sentimentale souvent tumultueuse : à peine le coup de foudre passé, c'est la déception... puis très vite le besoin de faire une nouvelle rencontre.

Those who fall in love with everyone they meet often have a tumultuous love life: no sooner have they fallen in love than they're disappointed... then very soon they feel the need to meet someone new.

avoir le cœur sur la main

> *"to have your heart on your hand"*
> = to have a heart of gold

● On the other hand, avoir du cœur au ventre, literally *to have your heart in your stomach*, means *to have guts.*

Fabrice dit qu'il ferait n'importe quoi par amitié. D'ailleurs tous ses amis disent qu'il a le cœur sur la main.
Fabrice says that he would do anything for the sake of friendship. All his friends say that he has a heart of gold.

être dans les petits papiers de quelqu'un

> *"to be in somebody's small papers"*
> = to be in somebody's good books

Personne ne doute qu'il aura le poste : il est dans les petits papiers de la directrice.
No one is in any doubt that he will get the job: he is in the director's good books.

avoir un Polichinelle dans le tiroir *(informal)*

"to have Punch in the drawer"
= to have a bun in the oven

● But be careful: **faire le Polichinelle** means *to act the buffoon.*

Toutes mes copines ont un Polichinelle dans le tiroir et ne parlent que de leur grossesse alors que moi je suis célibataire : pas facile de trouver des sujets de conversation !
All my female friends have a bun in the oven and talk of nothing but their pregnancies. I am single though, so it's not easy to find topics of conversation!

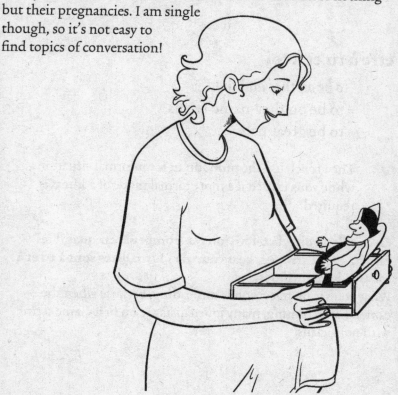

prendre son pied avec quelqu'un (informal)

"to take one's foot with somebody"
= to get your kicks with somebody
= to have it off with somebody

Son mari prenait son pied avec sa secrétaire pendant qu'elle était à la maison à s'occuper des enfants.
Her husband was having it off with his secretary while she was busy at home with the children.

être à tu et à toi

"to be on thee and thou"
= to be on first-name terms
= to be great pals

The French use the pronoun **tu** for informal situations, while **vous** is used if a more formal mode of address is required.

Ce que l'on voit à la télévision est trompeur, car quand les caméras sont arrêtées, beaucoup de journalistes sont à tu et à toi avec les politiques.
What you see on television is misleading, because when the cameras stop filming, many journalists are on first-name terms with politicians.

être unis comme les doigts de la main

> "*to be joined like the fingers of the hand*"
> = to be joined at the hip
> = to be very close

C'est l'histoire de trois frères unis comme les doigts de la main et que le destin allait séparer.
This is the story of three brothers who were once very close, but were destined to go their separate ways.

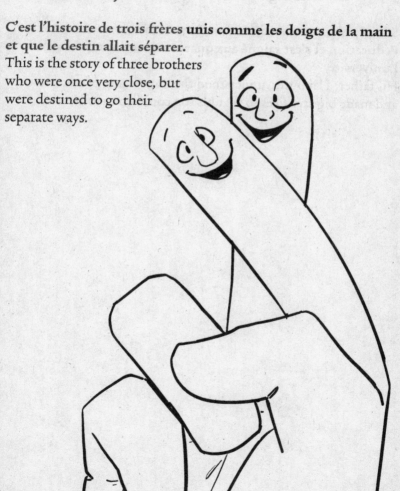

se saigner aux quatre veines

"to bleed yourself through four veins"
= to bleed yourself dry
= to make big sacrifices

Son père, un ouvrier, était conscient de l'importance de l'éducation et **s'est saigné aux quatre veines** pour qu'il aille à l'université.

His father, a labourer, understood the importance of education and made big sacrifices so that his son could go to university.

Argument, conflict, help
and cooperation

être pendu aux basques de quelqu'un (informal)

"to be hanging onto somebody's clothes"
= to stick to somebody like glue

● The French term, **les basques**, referred to lengths of
material which in times past hung down from the waist
like a kind of skirt.

**J'avais six ans de moins que ma sœur et j'étais toujours pendu à
ses basques, ce qui a fini par l'agacer.**
I was six years younger than my sister and
I used to stick to her like glue, which
ended up getting on her nerves.

se renvoyer la balle

> *"to send back the ball to each other"*
> = to try to pass the buck

● The idea here comes from sports where a ball is passed between players.

Comme d'habitude personne ne veut être tenu responsable du déficit et les deux partis se renvoient la balle.
As usual nobody wants to be held responsible for the deficit and the two parties try to pass the buck.

le torchon brûle

> *"the torch is burning"*
> = there is conflict

● Nowadays the French word **torchon** means *cloth* or *tea towel*, but in this expression it refers to a torch.

Depuis cette affaire d'espionnage, le torchon brûle entre les deux pays, qui ont rappelé leurs ambassadeurs ce matin.
The spy scandal has caused a serious falling-out between the two countries and they both recalled their ambassadors this morning.

tenir la dragée haute à quelqu'un

"to hold the sugared almond high for somebody"

= to hold out on somebody

= to stand up to somebody

Ici dans le stade, les supporters sont abasourdis : une équipe d'amateurs **tient la dragée haute à** un club de foot coté en Bourse !

The fans here in the stadium are stunned: a team of amateurs is standing up to a football club which is listed on the stock exchange!

rester en carafe *(informal)*

"to stay in the decanter"

= to be left stranded

= to be left high and dry

Similarly **tomber en carafe** means *to break down* or *to get stuck*.

La voiture ne voulait plus démarrer et il n'y avait pas moyen d'appeler une dépanneuse : on **est restés** six heures **en carafe** sur le bord de la route !

The car would not start and there was no way of calling a breakdown lorry: we were left stranded on the roadside for six hours!

avoir une dent contre quelqu'un

> *"to have a tooth against somebody"*
> = to have a grudge against somebody

● Also garder une dent contre quelqu'un. The Italians go one step further and talk about the tooth being poisoned.

Avec les efforts qu'elle fait pour ne pas me dire bonjour, elle doit forcément **avoir une dent contre moi** ; ce que je ne sais pas, c'est pourquoi.
From the efforts she makes to avoid saying hello to me, she really must have a grudge against me; what I don't know is why.

donner du fil à retordre à quelqu'un

> *"to give thread to twist again to somebody"*
> = to make life difficult for somebody

Les dialogues qui mélangent plusieurs dialectes italiens **ont donné** beaucoup **de fil à retordre** au traducteur.
Dialogue which mixes together several Italian dialects made life difficult for the translator.

se regarder en chiens de faïence

"to look at each other like china dogs"

= to glare at one another
= to be on hostile terms

The image here is of a pair of china ornaments set at either end of the mantelpiece, a common sight in past times.

Une situation qui rappelle la guerre froide, quand les deux superpuissances se regardaient en chiens de faïence.
A situation reminiscent of the Cold War, when the two superpowers were on hostile terms.

poser un lapin à quelqu'un (informal)

"to set down a rabbit for somebody"

= to stand somebody up

The French term **lapin** has long had an association with doing something without paying, or not fulfilling one's obligations.

J'avais rendez-vous avec Édith mais elle **m'a posé un lapin.** Je rentre chez moi.
I had a date with Édith but she has stood me up. I'm going home.

mettre la main à la pâte

"to put your hand to the dough"

= to lend a hand

= to muck in

Pour la fête de fin d'année, tout le monde **met la main à la pâte** : les professeurs décorent la salle, les enfants préparent une pièce de théâtre et les parents font des gâteaux.
For the end-of-year celebrations, everybody mucks in: the teachers decorate the hall, the children prepare a play and the parents make cakes.

couper l'herbe sous le pied de quelqu'un

"to cut the grass under somebody's feet"

= to cut the ground from under somebody's feet

= to pull the rug out from under somebody's feet

En sortant son modèle de voiture électrique deux mois avant ses concurrents, la marque espère leur couper l'herbe sous le pied.
By bringing out its electric car two months ahead of its competitors, the company hopes to cut the ground from under their feet.

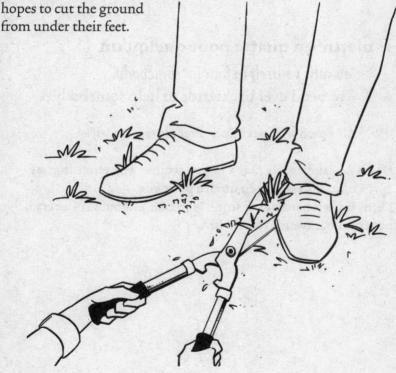

chercher midi à quatorze heures

> *"to look for midday at two o'clock"*
> = to complicate the issue

Inutile de chercher midi à quatorze heures, vous grillez le feu rouge, vous avez une amende !
No need to complicate the issue: if you go through a red light, you get a fine.

se mettre en quatre pour quelqu'un

> *"to split yourself in four for somebody"*
> = to bend over backwards to help somebody

Also used with **se couper**, literally *to cut oneself up*.

Denis a beaucoup de mal à ne pas trouver Hortense ingrate – après tout, il s'est mis en quatre pour elle.
Denis finds it hard not to think Hortense ungrateful – after all, he bent over backwards to help her.

c'est un panier de crabes

"it's a basket of crabs"

= they're always fighting among themselves

= they're always at each other's throats

Lassée du monde de la haute couture qu'elle décrit comme un panier de crabes, elle se retire à la campagne pour se consacrer à ses enfants et à l'écriture.

Weary of the world of haute couture in which she says everybody is at each other's throats, she is retiring to the country to devote herself to her children and to writing.

une tempête dans un verre d'eau

"a storm in a glass of water"

= a storm in a teacup

= a lot of fuss about nothing

Cette découverte que le scientifique qualifie de révolution pourrait n'être qu'**une tempête dans un verre d'eau.**
This discovery, which the scientist describes as revolutionary, could just be a lot of fuss about nothing.

Telling off, praise, critics and criticism

remonter les bretelles à quelqu'un (informal)

"to pull up somebody's braces"
= to give somebody a severe dressing down

⬤ The image here is similar to that of taking someone by the collar.

A la réunion, les chefs de projet risquent de se faire **remonter les bretelles** : le budget a triplé et la livraison a maintenant dix mois de retard !
At the meeting, the project managers are in danger of getting a severe dressing down: the budget has tripled and delivery is now ten months overdue!

tirer à boulets rouges sur quelqu'un

"to fire with red balls at somebody"
= to lay into somebody

● Cannon balls are one thing, but cannon balls heated to extreme temperatures are even worse.

Certains parents d'élèves passent leur temps à tirer à boulets rouges sur les professeurs sans connaître les difficultés qu'ils rencontrent.
Some pupils' parents spend their time laying into the teachers without knowing the difficulties they are up against.

être dans le collimateur de quelqu'un (informal)

"to be in somebody's telescopic sight"
= to be on somebody's hit list

L'entreprise est dans le collimateur des protecteurs des animaux depuis que des images de ses abattoirs ont été diffusées.
The business has been on the animal-welfare groups' hit list since pictures of its slaughterhouses were shown.

mettre quelqu'un en boîte (informal)

"*to put somebody in a box*"
= to pull somebody's leg

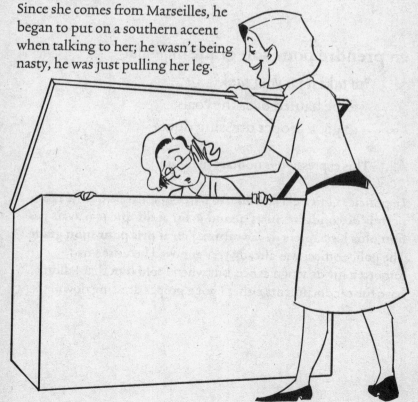

● You can also say *se payer la tête de quelqu'un*, literally *to buy yourself somebody's head*.

Comme elle vient de Marseille, il s'est mis à imiter l'accent du sud pour lui parler ; ça n'avait rien de méchant, c'était juste pour la mettre en boîte.

Since she comes from Marseilles, he began to put on a southern accent when talking to her; he wasn't being nasty, he was just pulling her leg.

faire des gorges chaudes de quelque chose

"to make hot throats of something"

= to laugh at something

Comme d'habitude, les journaux à scandale **font des gorges chaudes** d'un événement malheureux qui relève avant tout de la vie privée.

As usual, the tabloids are sniggering about an unfortunate incident which belongs entirely to somebody's private life.

en prendre pour son grade *(informal)*

"to take it for your rank"

= to be hauled over the coals

= to get a proper dressing down

This expression is military in origin.

Le policier était déjà très énervé parce que j'avais oublié mon permis de conduire, mais quand je lui ai dit que je n'avais pas non plus les papiers de la voiture, **j'en ai pris pour mon grade**.

The police officer was already very annoyed because I had forgotten my driving licence, but when I told him that I didn't have the car documents either I got a proper dressing down.

c'est la fin des haricots (informal)

> "it's the end of the beans"
> = that's the last straw

Being relatively cheap, beans and pulses were an important part of the diet of poorer people. When you ran out of them, it was a disaster!

On était perdus, la nuit tombait et il pleuvait ; quand j'ai vu qu'on n'avait plus d'essence, je me suis dit : c'est la fin des haricots.

We were lost, it was getting dark and it was raining; when I realized that we had run out of petrol I thought to myself: that's the last straw.

donner des noms d'oiseau à quelqu'un

> "to give somebody birds' names"
> = to call somebody names

Au parlement le débat a été agité : certains députés se sont même donné des noms d'oiseaux.

In parliament the debate was very heated: some members even called each other names.

être fait comme un rat *(informal)*

"to be done for like a rat"
= to be in for it
= to have no way out

L'ennemi nous encerclait et il n'y avait aucun espoir de recevoir de l'aide : nous **étions faits comme des rats.**
We were surrounded and there was no hope of getting help: we had no way out.

passer un savon à quelqu'un *(informal)*

"to scrub somebody with a bar of soap"
= to give somebody a telling-off

Quand elle a vu le dessin sur le mur à côté d'Olivier, la prof **lui a passé un savon.**
The teacher gave Olivier a telling-off when she saw the drawing on the wall next to him.

avaler des couleuvres (informal)

"to swallow grass snakes"

= to accept something against your will

= to have something forced on you

● This expression can also mean *to swallow a lie or to be taken in.* The alternative wording is even worse: **avaler des boas !**

L'an dernier les impôts ont augmenté et maintenant on leur annonce l'ouverture d'un incinérateur : les habitants de la commune en ont assez d'avaler des couleuvres.

Last year taxes went up, and now they've announced the opening of a new incinerator: the locals are fed up of having things forced upon them.

Mistakes, shame and embarrassment

mettre la charrue avant les bœufs

"to put the plough in front of the oxen"

= to put the cart before the horse

Ton projet de restaurant est intéressant mais tu mets la charrue avant les bœufs : avant de penser au menu, va voir ton banquier !

Your restaurant project is interesting but you are putting the cart before the horse: before thinking about the menu, go and see your bank manager!

être le dindon de la farce (informal)

"to be the turkey in the farce"
= to be duped
= to be taken for a ride

A more informal expression would be être le pigeon, literally meaning to be the pigeon.

Il est de plus en plus difficile de comparer les offres de téléphonie mobile et, comme d'habitude, le consommateur a le sentiment d'être le dindon de la farce.

It is increasingly difficult to compare all the different offers from the mobile phone networks and, as usual, it's the consumers who feel they are being taken for a ride.

avoir bon dos (informal)

"to have a good back"
= to take the blame

This expression can be used both of a person and of an enterprise or undertaking.

Les jeunes ont bon dos : à chaque fois qu'il y a du bruit dans le quartier on les accuse, mais dimanche dernier la musique venait du club du troisième âge !

Young people always get the blame: whenever there's noise in the neighbourhood it's assumed to be their fault, but last Sunday the music was coming from the senior citizens' club!

tomber dans le panneau (informal)

"to fall in the net"

= to walk right into the trap

= to fall for it

This expression has nothing to do with signs or notices. The word **panneau** here refers to the net in which hunters used to catch their prey.

Si vous recevez un courriel vous demandant votre numéro de carte bancaire, ne tombez pas dans le panneau !

If you receive an email asking you for your bank card number, don't fall for it!

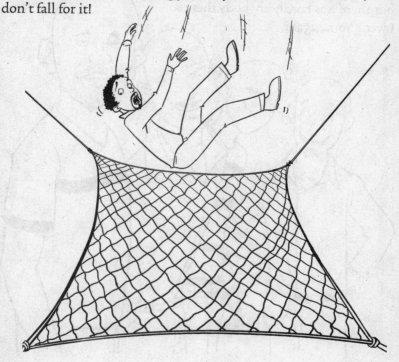

trois pelés et un tondu (informal)

"three bald people and one with closely-cropped hair"
= hardly anyone

The baldness referred to here would have been caused by a condition of the scalp thought to be contagious. Therefore a gathering of people with this condition wouldn't attract anyone else!

Je suis passé à la fête de Cécile hier soir mais il n'y avait que trois pelés et un tondu, alors je suis rentré chez moi.
I went to Cécile's party yesterday evening but there was hardly anybody there so I went home again.

être la cinquième roue du carrosse (informal)
   "to be the fifth wheel of the coach"
   = to feel like a spare part

J'ai quitté mon travail car j'avais l'impression d'**être la
cinquième roue du carrosse** : je me sentais inutile et on ne me
demandait jamais mon avis.
I left my job because I felt like a spare part: I felt useless and no
one ever asked me my opinion.

Knowledge, intelligence, ignorance and understanding

être à côté de la plaque (informal)

"to be to the side of the target"

= to be clueless

Benoît est très gentil mais il **est un peu à côté de la plaque** ; on habite ici depuis un an, et à chaque fois qu'il nous rend visite, il sonne chez les voisins d'en face.

Benoît is very nice, but a bit clueless; we've been living here a year and every time he visits us he rings the bell of the neighbours opposite.

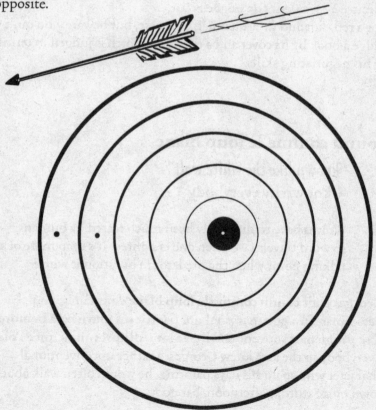

l'habit ne fait pas le moine

> *"the habit does not make the monk"*
> = appearances can be deceptive
> = you can't judge a book by its cover

● This proverbial expression also exists in Spanish and Italian.

Pour un commercial, le costume cravate est bien sûr de rigueur, mais attention : l'habit ne fait pas le moine et sa vraie valeur se mesure à ses talents de négociateur.
For a rep, suit and tie are a must, of course, but beware: you can't judge a book by its cover and a rep's true worth is judged in terms of his negotiating skills.

connu comme le loup blanc

> *"known like the white wolf"*
> = known by everybody

● Wolves have traditionally been much feared by humans, so word travels fast when one is sighted. It's even more of a talking point when the predator in question is white.

Georges était connu comme le loup blanc dans la région : personnage un peu marginal qui passait ses journées à peindre, il se promenait souvent en ville le samedi après-midi, pieds nus.
Everybody in the area knew Georges: a rather unconventional character who spent his days painting, he would often walk about town on a Saturday afternoon, barefoot.

ne pas être tombé de la dernière pluie

" *not to have fallen in the last rain*"

= not to be born yesterday

Ce n'est pas la peine de s'inquiéter : Thomas n'est pas **tombé de la dernière pluie**, il peut très bien se débrouiller tout seul.

There is no need to worry: Thomas was not born yesterday, he can fend for himself perfectly well.

ne pas savoir si c'est du lard ou du cochon
(informal)

"*not to know if it is bacon or pork*"

= not to know where you are

The idea here is that it is very difficult to tell between two things which are very closely related.

Il m'a dit qu'il va peut-être repeindre les volets en rose. Il l'a dit en plaisantant, mais on **ne sait jamais si c'est du lard ou du cochon** avec lui, donc je m'attends à tout.

He told me he might paint the shutters pink. He said it jokingly but you never know where you are with him so I am prepared for anything.

en connaître un rayon (informal)

"to know your shop counter"
= to be really clued up

Si tu veux des conseils pour ton nouvel appareil photo, tu devrais demander à Raphaëlle : elle **en connaît un rayon** sur le sujet.
If you want some advice about your new camera, you ought to ask Raphaëlle: she is really clued up on the subject.

un secret de Polichinelle

"a Punch secret"
= an open secret

Punch the puppet talks non-stop, so he is quite unable to keep anything secret.

Ahmed sort avec Marie ? Mais c'est **un secret de Polichinelle**, voyons, tout le monde sait ça. Ils sortent ensemble depuis deux ans !
Ahmed is going out with Marie? But that's an open secret: everybody knows about it. They've been going out together for two years!

tirer les vers du nez à quelqu'un (informal)

"to pull the worms from somebody's nose"

= to worm information out of somebody

Certains enfants parlent peu de ce qu'ils font à l'école ; leurs parents doivent **leur tirer les vers du nez.**

Some children don't talk much about what they do at school; their parents have to worm information out of them.

Looks, appearance, beauty and vanity

avoir la chair de poule

> *"to have chicken flesh"*

= to have goose pimples/gooseflesh

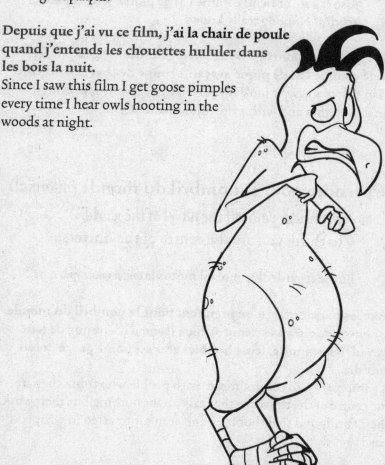

You can also say **donner la chair de poule**, meaning *to give goose pimples.*

Depuis que j'ai vu ce film, j'ai la chair de poule quand j'entends les chouettes hululer dans les bois la nuit.
Since I saw this film I get goose pimples every time I hear owls hooting in the woods at night.

être ficelé comme l'as de pique *(informal)*

"to be tied up like the ace of spades"
= to be dressed any old how
= to be wearing terrible clothes

● Also fagoté or fichu comme l'as de pique. Why the ace of spades? Nobody really knows.

Ce n'est pas toujours facile de se voir sur des vieilles photos, **ficelé comme l'as de pique** avec une coupe de cheveux ridicule.
It isn't always easy to look at yourself in old photos, wearing terrible clothes and with a ridiculous haircut.

se prendre pour le nombril du monde *(informal)*

"to consider yourself the navel of the world"
= to think you are the centre of the universe

● But se regarder le nombril means *to contemplate your navel.*

Avec les personnes qui **se prennent pour le nombril du monde**, la communication est impossible : ils ne parlent que de leur travail, leur famille, leurs hobbies et n'écoutent pas ce qu'on leur dit.
It's impossible to communicate with people who think they are the centre of the universe: they talk about nothing but their work, their family and their hobbies, and aren't interested in what you have to say.

être tiré à quatre épingles

"to be stretched by four pins"

= to be all dressed up

The idea here is that clothing that is stretched out and pinned at each corner has no creases and is at its neatest.

En voyant cet homme bien coiffé, rasé de près et **tiré à quatre épingles**, je n'ai pas tout de suite reconnu mon vieux copain Momo.

When I saw this man who had a good haircut, and was clean-shaven and all dressed up, I didn't at first recognize my old mate Momo.

faire la mouche du coche

"to be the coachman's fly"

= to fuss around self-importantly

Dans les cuisines du restaurant, Chantal, la femme du patron, **fait la mouche du coche** au milieu des employés qui préparent les plats.

In the restaurant kitchen, Chantal, the boss's wife, fusses around self-importantly amid the staff who are preparing the dishes.

être long comme un jour sans pain

> "to be as long as a day without bread"
> = to be endless

Pour pouvoir utiliser ce programme il faut lire la documentation, qui est longue comme un jour sans pain.
To be able to use this program you have to read endless documentation.

se mettre sur son trente et un

> "to put yourself on your thirty-one"
> = to get all dressed up
> = to get all dressed up to the nines

● Why thirty-one is such a special number is anybody's guess.

Ce soir, Enzo a rendez-vous avec Johanna : il s'est mis sur son trente et un et part la rejoindre, un énorme bouquet de fleurs à la main.
Enzo has a date with Johanna this evening: he is all dressed up and is going off to meet her with an enormous bunch of flowers in his hand.

jeter de la poudre aux yeux de quelqu'un

"to throw powder in the eyes of somebody"
= to try and impress somebody

Also note the expression *c'est de la poudre aux yeux*, meaning *it's all just for show*.

Pour les défenseurs de la nature, le ministre jette de la poudre aux yeux en proposant ces mesures démagogiques.
According to conservationists, the minister is trying to impress people by proposing these populist measures.

Madness, foolishness and stupidity

avoir une araignée au plafond (informal)

"to have a spider on the ceiling"

= to have bats in the belfry

= to have a screw loose

The idea here is that spiders thrive in neglected places, untroubled by human attention.

Quand il a commencé à parler tout seul, on a compris qu'il avait une araignée au plafond.

When he began to talk to himself, we realized he had a screw loose.

être bête comme ses pieds (informal)

"to be as stupid as your feet"
= to be too stupid for words
= to be thick as a brick

Feet don't always get a very good press: *faire quelque chose comme un pied* means *to be useless at doing something*.

Il est bête comme ses pieds : ça fait quinze fois qu'on lui explique, il n'a toujours pas compris.
He is too stupid for words: that's fifteen times he's had it explained, but he still doesn't understand.

comme les moutons de Panurge

"like Panurge's sheep"
= like sheep

Panurge, in Rabelais' work, throws one of his sheep into the sea – and all the rest follow.

Le problème des voyages organisés c'est que l'on visite les mêmes endroits que les autres, on mange dans les mêmes restaurants que les autres ... Finalement on se comporte comme des moutons de Panurge !
The problem with package holidays is that you visit the same places as everybody else and you eat in the same restaurants as everybody else: you end up behaving like sheep!

péter les plombs *(informal)*

"*to blow the fuses*"

= to flip your lid

Quand il a vu la rayure sur la portière de sa nouvelle voiture, il a complètement **pété les plombs** et s'est mis à hurler comme un fou.

When he saw the scratch on the door of his new car, he completely flipped his lid and started to yell like a madman.

vendre la peau de l'ours avant de l'avoir tué

> *"to sell the bear's skin before you have killed it"*
> = to count your chickens before they are hatched

This idiom is often shortened to **vendre la peau de l'ours** which matches the English phrase *to count your chickens*.

Nous pensons avoir de bonnes chances de remporter le marché, mais il ne faut pas vendre la peau de l'ours avant de l'avoir tué : la concurrence est rude.
We think we have a good chance of getting the deal but we mustn't count our chickens before they are hatched: the competition is tough.

se lever du pied gauche

> *"to get out of bed with the left foot"*
> = to get out of bed on the wrong side

Annick s'était encore levée du pied gauche et ne m'a pas adressé la parole de la matinée.
Annick got out of bed on the wrong side again and hasn't said a word to me all morning.

il n'a pas inventé la poudre

"he didn't invent gunpowder"
= he's not the sharpest tool in the box
= he's no bright spark

● Instead of la **poudre** you can say l'eau chaude (*hot water*) or le fil à couper le beurre (*the wire for cutting butter*).

A l'école on disait qu'**il n'avait pas inventé la poudre,** alors aujourd'hui on a de la peine à croire qu'il soit devenu milliardaire !
At school he wasn't considered to be the sharpest tool in the box, so today it is hard to believe that he has become a multimillionaire!

Relationships, similarities and differences

ne pas arriver à la cheville de quelqu'un

"not to reach somebody's ankle"

= not to be a patch on somebody

● Note also the idiom **être en cheville avec quelqu'un**, meaning *to be in cahoots with somebody.*

Le guitariste a été remplacé par un autre qui ne lui arrive pas à la cheville ; depuis, le groupe n'a plus aucun succès.
The guitarist was replaced by someone who is not a patch on him; since then the band hasn't had any success at all.

c'est bonnet blanc et blanc bonnet

"it's bonnet white and white bonnet"
= it amounts to the same thing
= there's nothing to choose between the two

Thierry dit comme beaucoup de ses concitoyens que les deux partis "c'est bonnet blanc et blanc bonnet", c'est pourquoi il n'ira pas voter dimanche prochain.
Like many of his fellow citizens, Thierry says there's nothing to choose between the two parties, and that is why he is not going to vote next Sunday.

devoir une fière chandelle à quelqu'un

"to owe somebody a proud candle"
= to be terribly indebted to somebody

This refers to the religious ritual of lighting a candle to give thanks to God.

Je dois une fière chandelle à Marco ; il m'a logé le temps que je trouve un appartement et a toujours été là pour moi. Je ne l'oublierai pas.
I am terribly indebted to Marco; he put me up while I found a flat and has always been there for me. I'll never forget him.

casser les pieds à quelqu'un (informal)

"to break somebody's feet"

= to get on somebody's nerves

La voisine me casse les pieds tous les soirs depuis deux ans avec son violon. J'ai décidé de déménager.
My neighbour has been getting on my nerves with her violin-playing every night for two years. I've decided to move house.

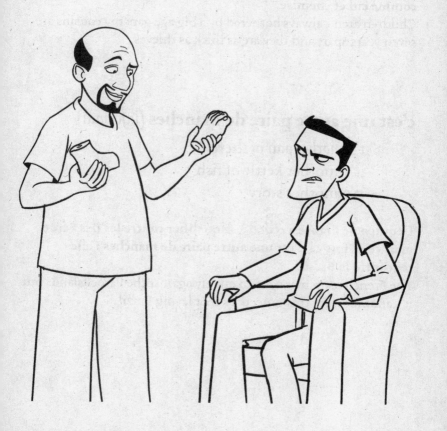

être comme cul et chemise (informal)

>   *"to be like backside and shirt"*
>   = to be as thick as thieves

Shirt tails used to be longer than they are now!

Les différences d'âge ne sont pas toujours un problème pour les enfants : mes cousins ont sept ans de différence et ils sont comme cul et chemise.
Children aren't always bothered by a big age gap: my cousins are seven years apart and they are as thick as thieves.

c'est une autre paire de manches (informal)

>   *"it's another pair of sleeves"*
>   = it's another kettle of fish
>   = it's another story

L'équipe de France a réussi à se qualifier contre les îles Féroé, mais cette fois-ci, c'est une autre paire de manches : elle rencontre le Brésil.
The French team managed to qualify against the Faroe Islands but it's another story this time: they are playing Brazil.

Problems, difficulties, the possible and the impossible

en deux coups de cuillère à pot (informal)

"in two scoops of a ladle"
= in two shakes of a lamb's tail
= in no time at all

● Also en trois coups de cuillère à pot. Whether it's two or three scoops, the idea is that you are ladling out food from a pot very quickly.

Avec l'aide de Mathieu et de ses copains rugbymen, on a déplacé le piano en deux coups de cuillère à pot.
With the help of Mathieu and his
rugby-playing mates, we shifted
the piano in no time at all.

ne pas être sorti de l'auberge

> *"not to have got out of the inn"*
> = not to be out of the woods

● In this expression, the French word **auberge**, meaning *inn*, is actually slang for *prison*.

Mon GPS est cassé, alors si on ne trouve pas de carte, on n'est pas sortis de l'auberge !

My sat nav is broken, so unless we find a map, we're not out of the woods yet!

il n'y a pas de quoi fouetter un chat

> *"there is nothing to whip a cat about"*
> = it is only a trifle
> = it's nothing to make a fuss about

● As in English, the French language has many expressions to do with cats.

Il a juste volé un paquet de bonbons, il n'y a pas de quoi fouetter un chat.

He's only stolen a bag of sweets: it's not worth making a fuss about.

tiré par les cheveux

> "*pulled by the hair*"
> = far-fetched

● The idea here is of something forced or improbable.

Les acteurs jouent bien, mais le scénario est vraiment tiré par les cheveux : on n'y croit à aucun moment !
The acting is good but the script is really far-fetched: you don't believe it for a minute!

la croix et la bannière

> "*the cross and the banner*"
> = the devil's own job
> = an uphill struggle

● This expression describes the organizational nightmare that was medieval processions. These followed a strict hierarchy, with local dignitaries and members of the clergy at the head of the parade, behind the cross, and the rest of the procession following behind various banners.

Votre adolescent passe ses nuits sur internet ? C'est la croix et la bannière pour le tirer du lit le matin ? Voici quelques conseils pour vous.
Does your teenager spend all night on the Internet? Is it an uphill struggle to get him out of bed in the morning? Here is some advice for you.

être dans de beaux draps (informal)

"to be in beautiful sheets"
= to be in a right fix
= to be in a right mess

You can also say **être dans de sales draps**, literally *to be in dirty sheets*.

Quand on est revenu de la plage, la voiture avait disparu avec nos papiers, notre argent et nos vêtements : on était dans de beaux draps !
When we got back from the beach the car had disappeared, along with our documents, our money and our clothes: we were in a right mess!

il y a de l'eau dans le gaz (informal)

"there is water in the gas"
= things aren't going too smoothly

This image comes from the kitchen, when water boils over onto the lighted gas on the hob.

On dirait qu'il y a de l'eau dans le gaz entre les réceptionnistes : elles ne se sont pas parlé de la journée.
It looks like things aren't going too smoothly between the receptionists: they haven't spoken to each other all day.

vouloir le beurre et l'argent du beurre

"to want the butter and the money for the butter"
= to want to have your cake and eat it

A staple ingredient in French cooking, butter features in a
number of expressions.

**Dans l'ensemble, les clients sont corrects, mais il y a toujours
ceux qui en veulent plus en payant moins, qui veulent le beurre
et l'argent du beurre, quoi !**
On the whole customers are ok but there are always those who
want more for less, who want to have their cake and eat it.

ne pas pouvoir être au four et au moulin

"not to be able to be at the oven and at the mill"
= not to be able to be in two places at once
= not to be able to do everything at once

⬤ Once you had ground your grain, you had to bake your bread, but you couldn't do both things at the same time.

Depuis qu'elle est maman, Anne se rend compte qu'elle ne peut pas être au four et au moulin et elle a dû renoncer à certaines activités.
Since becoming a mum, Anne has realized that she can't do everything and she has had to give up certain things.

veiller au grain

"to look out for squalls"
= to watch out for problems

⬤ The image here is of a sailor keeping a lookout for signs of a storm at sea.

Certains usagers du site publient des messages douteux, mais heureusement le modérateur veille au grain.
Some users of the site post dodgy messages, but fortunately the moderator watches out for problems.

marcher comme sur des roulettes (informal)

"*to work as if on casters*"
= to be plain sailing

Si vous suivez mes instructions, tout **marchera comme sur des roulettes** et nous serons tous riches.

If you follow my instructions, everything will be plain sailing and we will all be rich.

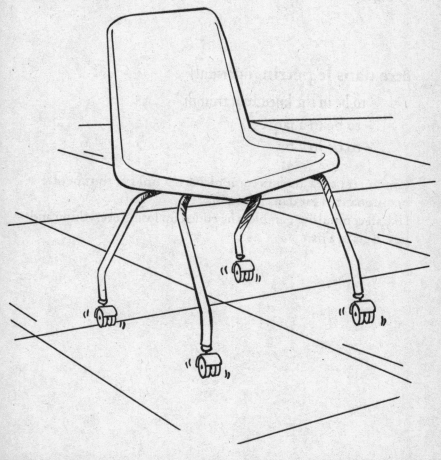

ce n'est pas la mer à boire (informal)

"it's not as if you're having to drink the sea"
= it's no big deal

Pour le test d'entrée, il y a un QCM et un entretien d'un quart d'heure. Ce n'est pas la mer à boire.
For the entry test, there is a multiple-choice paper and a 15-minute interview. It's no big deal.

être dans le pétrin (informal)

"to be in the kneading trough"
= to be in a jam
= to be in a fix

Comme tous les joueurs compulsifs, il a fini par tout perdre et maintenant, il est dans le pétrin.
Like all compulsive gamblers he ended up losing everything and now he is in a fix.

Orders, obedience, control
and equality

peigner la girafe *(informal)*
  "to comb the giraffe"
  = to do a pointless task

● What could be more pointless than combing a giraffe!

Après trois ans de ce travail où j'étais payé une misère à peigner la girafe, j'ai trouvé un autre poste. Je ne gagne pas plus, mais au moins je sers à quelque chose.
After three years in this job where I was paid a pittance for doing a pointless task, I found another post. I don't earn any more but at least I'm doing something useful.

mener quelqu'un à la baguette

"to lead somebody with the baton"
= to rule somebody with a rod of iron

● The baguette in question is not edible!

L'école de la commune est dirigée par Nicole, une petite femme énergique qui **mène** tout le monde **à la baguette**.
The head of the village school is Nicole, a small energetic woman who rules everybody with a rod of iron.

compter pour du beurre *(informal)*

"to count for butter"
= to count for nothing

● Butter enriches both French cuisine and French idioms.

Vous allez garder tout l'argent pour vous ? Et nous alors, on compter pour du beurre ?
You're going to keep all the money for yourself? And what about us, do we count for nothing?

obéir au doigt et à l'œil

"to obey the finger and the eye"
= to toe the line
= to do what you are told

This expression refers to the finger and eye of the person giving you the orders.

Les adeptes de la domotique veulent des maisons qui obéissent au doigt et à l'œil.
Home automation enthusiasts want houses that do what they're told.

tenir la jambe à quelqu'un *(informal)*

"to hold somebody's leg"
= to pin somebody down

If you hold on to somebody's leg and don't let go, they can't get very far.

Désolé d'être en retard ; je suis tombé sur un représentant qui m'a tenu la jambe, je n'arrivais pas à m'en débarrasser.
Sorry I'm late; I got pinned down by a rep and I couldn't get away.

se faire tirer l'oreille

> "to have your ear pulled"
> = to get a telling off

Les pays qui n'ont pas suffisamment réduit leurs émissions de CO_2 risquent de **se faire tirer l'oreille** au prochain sommet sur l'environnement.

Countries which have not made sufficient reductions in their CO_2 emissions are in danger of getting a telling off at the next environment summit.

faire la pluie et le beau temps

> "to make rain and shine"
> = to call the shots

Dans certaines villes, la mafia **fait la pluie et le beau temps** et la police n'intervient plus.

In some towns the mafia call the shots and the police don't even bother getting involved anymore.

faire la fine bouche

> *"to make a thin mouth"*
>
> = to turn your nose up

● A medieval French expression: the original form, **faire la petite bouche**, is no longer current.

On ne va pas faire la fine bouche, on n'a rien mangé depuis hier.

We're not going to turn our noses up: we haven't eaten a thing since yesterday.

pour des prunes (informal)

> "for plums"
> = for nothing

Tu veux dire que tous ces efforts n'ont servi à rien, qu'on a fait tout ça **pour des prunes** ?
You mean to say that all this effort was pointless, and we did all that for nothing?

ne pas quitter quelqu'un d'une semelle

> "not to leave somebody by the sole of a shoe"
> = not to leave somebody for a second
> = to be inseparable from somebody

● Quitter can be replaced by lâcher (to let go of).

Edmond et Geneviève se sont mariés il y a soixante ans et depuis ils **ne se sont pas quittés d'une semelle** : ils vont bientôt fêter leurs noces de diamant.
Edmond and Geneviève got married sixty years ago and they have been inseparable ever since: soon they'll be celebrating their diamond wedding anniversary.

cracher dans la soupe (informal)

"to spit in the soup"
= to bite the hand that feeds you

Il n'est pas fier d'avoir participé à cette émission de téléréalité, mais à l'époque il avait besoin d'argent et il ne voulait pas **cracher dans la soupe.**

He's not proud of the fact that he took part in this reality TV show but at the time he needed money and he didn't want to bite the hand that fed him.

Work, laziness, effort and ambition

avoir du pain sur la planche (informal)

"to have bread on the board"
= to have a lot to do
= to have a lot on your plate
= to have your work cut out

This expression used to indicate somebody had plenty of resources, but has since changed its meaning.

J'aimerais bien rester avec vous pour dîner, mais j'ai du pain sur la planche, il faut que je parte.
I would love to stay with you for dinner but I have a lot on my plate, I've got to go.

se mettre dans le bain

> "*to put yourself in the bath*"
> = to get into the swing of things
> = to warm up

Pour nous mettre dans le bain, nous allons faire un peu de calcul mental.
To warm up, we are going to do a bit of mental arithmetic.

c'est simple comme bonjour

> "*it's as simple as good morning*"
> = it's as easy as ABC

A more informal way of saying this in French would be **bête comme chou.**

Aujourd'hui, la recette du gratin dauphinois – vous allez voir, c'est simple comme bonjour.
Today, the recipe for dauphinoise potatoes – you'll see, it's as easy as ABC.

mettre les bouchées doubles

> *"to put in double mouthfuls"*
>
> = to put on a spurt
>
> = to work twice as hard

Les examens ne sont plus que dans deux semaines et les
étudiants **mettent les bouchées doubles** pour être prêts.
The exams are only two weeks away and the students are working
twice as hard to be ready for them.

être à la bourre *(informal)*

> *"to be in the stuffing"*
>
> = to be behind
>
> = to be late

Une fois de plus, Pierre n'avait pas entendu son réveil et il **était
à la bourre**.
Once again, Pierre hadn't heard his alarm clock and was late.

aller au charbon *(informal)*

> *"to go to the coal"*
> = to stick your neck out

Not to be confused with the idea in the English expression, *at the coal face*.

Quand il y a une crise, un conflit, une catastrophe, c'est le ministre concerné qui va au charbon.
When there is a crisis, a conflict or a disaster, it's the minister responsible who has to stick his neck out.

faire quelque chose les doigts dans le nez *(informal)*

> *"to do something with the fingers in your nose"*
> = to be able to do something standing on your head
> = to be able to do something with your eyes closed

A graphic way of showing that your hands are otherwise occupied!

Un prodige du piano, qui à l'âge de huit ans jouait Chopin les doigts dans le nez.
A piano prodigy who at the age of eight could play Chopin standing on his head.

avoir les dents longues

"to have long teeth"

= to be very ambitious

= to have your sights set high

This expression used to mean *to be hungry*, for obvious reasons. A humorous alternative is avoir les dents qui rayent le parquet, literally *to have teeth which scratch the wooden floor*.

Les employés les plus anciens se méfient parfois des jeunes : certains ont les dents longues et ne reculent devant rien pour se faire une place dans l'entreprise.
Sometimes the older employees distrust the younger ones: some are very ambitious and will stop at nothing to establish themselves in the company.

n'avoir pas froid aux yeux

> "not to have cold eyes"
> = to be adventurous

Ceux qui **n'ont pas froid aux yeux** seront comblés : saut à l'élastique, en parachute, canyoning sont au programme.
Those who are a bit more adventurous will be overjoyed: they can do bungee jumping, parachuting and canyoning.

faire des pieds et des mains pour obtenir quelque chose *(informal)*

> "to use feet and hands to get something"
> = to move heaven and earth to get something

De nombreux touristes qui avaient réservé leur hôtel et leur vol ont dû **faire des pieds et des mains** pour obtenir un visa à la dernière minute.
Many tourists who had reserved their hotel and flight had to move heaven and earth to obtain a visa at the last minute.

avoir un poil dans la main *(informal)*

"*to have a hair in your hand*"
= to be bone-idle

Au bout de trois mois, elle se rend compte que son assistante **a un poil dans la main** : elle arrive en retard, passe son temps au téléphone avec ses amis et ne fait absolument rien.
After three months, she realizes that her assistant is bone-idle: she arrives late, spends all her time on the phone to her friends and does absolutely nothing.

contre vents et marées

"*against winds and tides*"
= against all the odds

Au début, personne ne voulait de son projet de film ; il s'est battu **contre vents et marées** pour pouvoir le réaliser.
At the start, nobody wanted anything to do with his film project: he fought against all the odds in order to make it happen.

Change, continuity, risk and opportunity

avoir les deux pieds dans le même sabot

"to have both feet in the same clog"

= to sit back and wait for things to happen

● You can also say **rester les deux pieds dans le même sabot**.

Il est jeune mais il n'a pas les deux pieds dans le même sabot, il sait se débrouiller.

He's young but he doesn't sit back and wait for things to happen: he can manage things for himself.

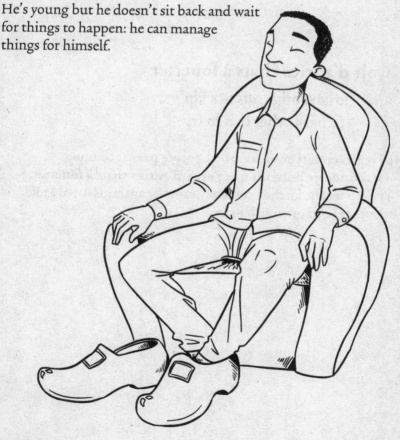

à tout bout de champ

"at every end of the field"
= all the time

Les amoureux de la langue française disent qu'il faut arrêter d'utiliser des mots anglais **à tout bout de champ**.
Lovers of the French language say that we must stop using English words all the time.

avoir d'autres chats à fouetter

"to have other cats to whip"
= to have other fish to fry

Le représentant en cuisines est encore passé ; comme d'habitude, je lui ai dit que j'avais **d'autres chats à fouetter**.
The rep for the kitchen company came by again; as usual I told him that I had other fish to fry.

en mettre sa main au feu

"*to put your hand into the fire over something*"
= to stake your life on something

● Also en mettre sa main à couper, literally *to put your hand in to be cut off.*

Je la reconnais, je sais que c'est elle, j'en mettrais ma main au feu !
I recognize her, I know it's her, I'd stake my life on it!

de fil en aiguille

> "from thread to needle"
> = gradually
> = eventually

● The image of a needle being threaded conveys the idea of a process taking place.

Au début, je ne savais pas qui était la personne avec Loïc, mais de fil en aiguille j'ai compris que c'était son compagnon.
At first I didn't know who the person with Loïc was but eventually I gathered that it was his partner.

changer son fusil d'épaule

> "to put your gun on the other shoulder"
> = to have a change of heart

● The image here is a military one, the soldier shifting his gun from one side to the other.

D'abord il envisageait de faire des études de sociologie, puis il a changé son fusil d'épaule et a choisi l'histoire.
To begin with he considered studying sociology, then he had a change of heart and chose history.

c'est reparti comme en quarante ! *(informal)*

> *"it's started again like in the year 1940!"*
> = here we go again!

● This refers to 1940, the start of WW2 in France. The idiom used to be **comme en quatorze** referring to 1914, the start of WW1.

Cinq ans après leur divorce, c'est reparti comme en quarante : ils se remarient !
Five years after their divorce, here we go again: they are getting remarried!

être réglé comme du papier à musique *(informal)*

> *"to be as neatly ruled as manuscript paper"*
> = to be as regular as clockwork

La vie de mon voisin est réglée comme du papier à musique : à six heures douze son réveil sonne , à sept heures cinq il ferme sa porte, à dix-huit heures quarante il rentre du travail.
My neighbour's life is as regular as clockwork: at 6.12am his alarm goes off; at 7.05am he shuts his door behind him; at 6.40pm he comes back from work.

Motion, travel, arrival and departure

faire une croix sur quelque chose (informal)

"to make a cross on something"
= to say goodbye to something
= to kiss something goodbye

○ This is similar to the idea in English of crossing something off a list.

J'ai reçu la facture du plombier : je peux faire une croix sur mon voyage au Pérou.
I've received the plumber's bill: I can kiss my trip to Peru goodbye.

filer à l'anglaise

> "*to run away in the English way*"
> = to make a getaway
> = to take French leave

● It seems that the French and the English feel the same about each other's manners!

Nous avons profité de la coupure d'électricité pour filer à l'anglaise.
We took advantage of the lights going out to make a getaway.

sur les chapeaux de roues (*informal*)

> "*on the hub caps*"
> = at top speed
> = like a shot

● A striking image – though it's hard to imagine how the car rights itself again!

Le théâtre commence la nouvelle année sur les chapeaux de roues, avec pas moins de quinze spectacles au programme pour le mois à venir.
The theatre starts at full speed in the New Year, with no less than fifteen shows on the programme for the coming month.

au diable

> *"with the devil"*
> = miles from anywhere
> = at the back of beyond

Les scientifiques vivent dans un poste d'observation **situé au diable**, accessible par hélicoptère seulement.
The scientists live in an observation post miles from anywhere, which is only accessible by helicopter.

prendre ses jambes à son cou

> *"to take your legs to your neck"*
> = to make a dash for it

Quand j'ai vu le taureau s'approcher, **j'ai pris mes jambes à mon cou.**
When I saw the bull coming, I made a dash for it.

prendre le large (informal)

> "to take the open sea"
> = to clear off
> = to make off

Another informal expression with a maritime connection is **mettre les voiles**, literally *to hoist the sails*.

L'employé **a pris le large** avec le contenu du coffre-fort et reste introuvable depuis lundi dernier.
The employee cleared off with the contents of the safe and has been nowhere to be found since last Monday.

se faire la malle (informal)

> "to pack your trunk"
> = to make yourself scarce
> = to scarper

Quand il est rentré chez lui, il y avait juste une lettre sur la table : c'était sa femme, elle s'**était fait la malle** avec son meilleur copain.
When he got home, there was just a letter on the table: it was his wife, she had scarpered with his best mate.

à tombeau ouvert

"with an open tomb"
= at breakneck speed

Le film se termine par une course-poursuite mémorable, où le héros roule à tombeau ouvert dans les rues de Marseille.
The film ends with a memorable car chase in which the hero drives at breakneck speed through the streets of Marseilles.

regagner ses pénates (*informal*)

"to go back to your household gods"
= to go home

The Penates were the household gods worshipped by the ancient Romans.

Déjà onze heures et demie : je suis fatigué, je vais regagner mes pénates.
11.30 already: I'm tired, I'm going to go home.

tomber à pic (*informal*)

"to land just right"
= to come at exactly the right time

Also used with **arriver** (*to arrive*). The image comes from the game of royal tennis and describes the ball landing in a certain spot to one player's advantage.

Tu tombes à pic ! J'avais justement besoin de ton aide.
You've come at exactly the right time! I could do with your help right now.

ne pas être aux pièces (informal)

> *"not to be on piecework"*
> = not to be in a rush

Prenez le temps de bien remplir le questionnaire, on n'est pas aux pièces.
Take your time to fill the questionnaire in properly, we're not in a rush.

prendre la poudre d'escampette (informal)

> *"to take running-away powder"*
> = to take to your heels
> = to skedaddle

● The word **escampette** comes from an old French word for flight or escape.

Ce matin, la cellule du gentleman cambrioleur était vide : il a pris la poudre d'escampette.
The gentleman burglar's cell was empty this morning: he's skedaddled.

Chance, surprise and the unexpected

être la douche écossaise (informal)

"to be a Scottish shower"

= to come as a bit of a shock

It is said that a Scottish shower runs alternately hot and cold.

Pour les employés de l'usine, c'est la douche écossaise : hier leur directeur les rassurait avec les bons résultats de l'entreprise, aujourd'hui ils apprennent la suppression de 200 emplois.
It's come as a bit of a shock for the factory workers: yesterday their manager was reassuring them with the company's strong results, today they're finding out that 200 jobs are to go.

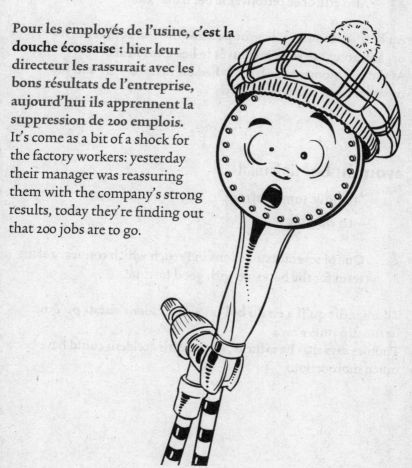

rester le bec dans l'eau (informal)

"to be left with your beak in the water"
= to be left in the lurch
= to be left high and dry

● Also être or se retrouver le bec dans l'eau.

Au dernier moment, le groupe a annulé son concert et les
organisateurs **se sont retrouvés le bec dans l'eau.**
At the last moment the band called off their concert and the
organizers were left in the lurch.

avoir du bol (informal)

"to have some bottom"
= to be lucky

● One of several expressions in French which connect a slang
term for the backside with good fortune.

Thomas dit qu'il **a eu du bol** car son accident aurait pu être
beaucoup plus grave.
Thomas says that he is lucky, because his accident could have been
much more serious.

il n'y a pas un chat (informal)

> "there isn't a cat"
> = there is no one at all
> = there is not a soul to be seen

● Where there are people, there are bound to be cats somewhere about. So no cats, no people.

Un dimanche soir de novembre dans une petite ville de province : il n'y a pas un chat.
A Sunday evening in November in a small provincial town: there is not a soul to be seen.

en boucher un coin à quelqu'un (informal)

> "to close somebody's mouth"
> = to render somebody speechless

● Here the French word, coin, does not have its common meaning *corner*, but refers to the mouth, which is speechless with astonishment.

Quand il m'a annoncé qu'il partait faire le tour du monde, ça m'en a bouché un coin.
When he told me that he was leaving to go round the world, I was speechless.

il n'y a pas le feu (informal)

"there is no fire"
= there's no panic

To make the point even more strongly you can also say il n'y a pas le feu au lac, literally *the lake is not on fire*.

Ce n'est pas la peine de courir, **il n'y a pas le feu**. Le film commence dans une heure.
There's no need to run, there's no panic. The film doesn't start for an hour.

jeter un pavé dans la mare

"to throw a cobblestone in the pond"
= to set the cat among the pigeons

L'écrivain **a jeté un pavé dans la mare** en refusant le prix littéraire, qu'il a qualifié de "mascarade".
The writer set the cat among the pigeons by turning down the literary prize, which he described as a farce.

tomber des nues

"*to fall from the clouds*"
= to be stunned
= to be flabbergasted

Quand je lui ai dit que la fête était annulée, Sophie est tombée des nues : personne ne l'avait mise au courant.
When I told her that the party had been cancelled, Sophie was stunned: nobody had told her.

finir en queue de poisson

> *"to end in a fish's tail"*
> = to come to an abrupt end

This expression originates in the mermaid myth: at first she appears to be human, but there is a surprise from the waist down.

L'histoire **finit en queue de poisson** : deux pages avant la fin, le héros disparaît sans qu'on sache pourquoi.
The story comes to an abrupt end: two pages before the end the hero disappears and you don't know why.

vingt-deux ! *(informal)*

> *"twenty-two!"*
> = watch out!

Why twenty-two? Nobody really knows!

Pendant que j'essaie de forcer la serrure, Paulo monte la garde. Tout d'un coup il crie "**Vingt-deux**, v'là les flics !" et s'enfuit en courant.
While I am trying to force the lock, Paulo is on guard. All of a sudden he shouts, 'Watch out, it's the cops!' and runs off.

Eating, drinking, drunkenness and excess

manger sur le pouce

"to eat on the thumb"

= to have a quick snack

= to snatch a bite to eat

À midi, les Français **mangent sur le pouce** comme la plupart de leurs voisins européens.

At lunchtime, the French have a quick snack, like most of their European neighbours.

pendre la crémaillère

"to hang the pot-hook"
= to have a housewarming party

In the old days, you would have attached your cooking pot onto your newly installed pot-hook, lit the fire, and invited the neighbours in to celebrate!

Ils ont emménagé dans leur nouvelle maison et pendent la crémaillère dans quinze jours.
They've moved into their new house and are having a house-warming party in a fortnight.

ne pas y aller avec le dos de la cuillère *(informal)*

"not to use the back of the spoon"
= not to go in for half-measures

To appreciate the sense of this expression, you don't actually have to try to eat soup with the spoon held the wrong way up.

Des milliers de figurants, un casting de rêve, les meilleurs spécialistes des effets spéciaux : à Hollywood, on n'y va pas avec le dos de la cuillère.
Thousands of extras, a dream cast, the best special effects specialists: in Hollywood, they don't go in for half-measures.

avoir la dalle (informal)

> "to have the throat"
> = to be starving

● But be careful: avoir la dalle en pente, literally *to have one's throat at a slope*, means *to be a bit of a boozer*.

Le frigo est vide. Arnaud devait avoir la dalle.
The fridge is empty. Arnaud must have been starving.

se rincer la dalle (informal)

> "to rinse your throat"
> = to wet your whistle

● This expression is used with any kind of drink, not just alcoholic ones.

Entre deux châteaux de la Loire, on mangeait dans des bons petits restaurants où l'on se rinçait la dalle avec des vins du coin... mémorable !
In between visiting two Loire valley châteaux, we ate in some great little restaurants where we wetted our whistles with local wines... unforgettable!

avoir l'estomac dans les talons

"to have your stomach in your heels"
= to be starving
= to be famished

You can also say **avoir un creux à l'estomac**, literally *to have a hole in your stomach*.

Ne négligez pas le petit-déjeuner : vous risquez **d'avoir l'estomac dans les talons** toute la matinée et de trop manger à midi.
Don't skimp on breakfast: you run the risk of being famished all morning and of eating too much at lunchtime.

avoir la gueule de bois (*informal*)

"to have a wooden mouth"
= to have a hangover

Quand on **a la gueule de bois**, la meilleure chose à faire est de boire beaucoup d'eau.
When you have a hangover, the best thing to do is to drink lots of water.

Directness, decisiveness
and expressing opinions

mi-figue mi-raisin

"half-fig half-grape"
= somewhat mixed

Leur réaction était **mi-figue mi-raisin. En tous cas ils n'avaient
pas l'air enthousiastes.**
Their reaction was somewhat mixed. In any event they didn't
seem keen.

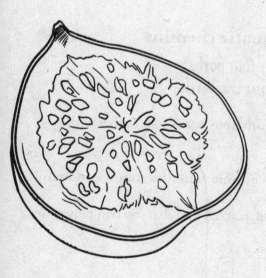

ça ne me fait ni chaud ni froid

> *"that makes me neither hot nor cold"*
> = I couldn't care less
> = it doesn't bother me

Sébastien s'évanouit quand il voit du sang. Moi, ça ne me fait ni chaud ni froid.
Sébastien faints when he sees blood. It doesn't bother me.

ne pas y aller par quatre chemins

> *"not to go there by four paths"*
> = not to beat about the bush

● If there is a direct path from A to B, why bother with another three?

N'y allez pas par quatre chemins : dites-lui simplement que vous ne l'aimez plus.
Don't beat about the bush: just tell him that you don't love him any more.

mettre son grain de sel *(informal)*

"to put in your grain of salt"

= to stick your oar in

= to put in your two cents

Greek people put in their tail and the Germans put in mustard.

À la fin de la réunion, tout le monde a voulu **mettre son grain de sel** et on ne comprenait plus rien à la discussion.

At the end of the meeting everyone wanted to stick their oar in, and it was impossible to make out the line of the argument.

regarder les choses par le petit bout de la lorgnette

"to look at things via the small end of the opera glasses"

= to take a very limited view of things

= to take a narrow view of things

Je lui ai dit d'arrêter de **regarder les choses par le petit bout de la lorgnette** ; il m'a répondu que c'est ma vision qui est étriquée.

I told him to stop taking a narrow view of things; he replied that it was my vision which was limited.

ne pas y aller de main morte (informal)

"not to use a dead hand"

= not to pull your punches

Il n'y est pas allé de main morte en critiquant les nouvelles mesures du gouvernement.
He didn't pull his punches when criticizing the new government measures.

il n'y a pas photo (informal)

"there's no photo"

= there's no question about it

This expression originated at the race track, where a photo finish indicates that the identity of the winning horse is not immediately obvious.

Il n'y a pas photo : l'équipe russe est meilleure.
There's no question about it: the Russian team is better.

enfoncer une porte ouverte

> "to break down an open door"
> = to state the obvious

Also enfoncer des portes ouvertes.

Pour un ministre de l'Environnement, dire qu'il faut protéger la nature, c'est enfoncer une porte ouverte.
For an Environment Minister, saying that we must protect nature is stating the obvious.

ne pas faire un pli *(informal)*

"*not to make a crease*"
= to be for sure
= sure enough

Je lui avais dit qu'il aurait des problèmes avec cette maison : ça n'a pas fait un pli, il y a des fuites d'eau partout !
I told him that he would have problems with this house: sure enough, there are leaks everywhere!

noyer le poisson

"*to drown the fish*"
= to evade the issue
= to sidestep the question

Arrêtez d'essayer de noyer le poisson et répondez-moi clairement : quand allez-vous me payer la facture ?
Stop trying to evade the issue and give me a clear answer: when are you going to pay my invoice?

ne pas tourner autour du pot

> *"not to turn around the pot"*
> = not to beat about the bush

Il n'a pas tourné autour du pot : il a dit qu'il a trouvé le repas infect.
He didn't beat about the bush: he said he found the meal revolting.

mettre la puce à l'oreille de quelqu'un

> *"to put the flea in somebody's ear"*
> = to get somebody thinking

Quand elle m'a dit de réserver mon samedi, ça m'a mis la puce à l'oreille, mais je ne me doutais pas qu'elle préparait un anniversaire-surprise.
When she told me to keep Saturday free it got me thinking, but I had no idea that she was planning a surprise birthday party.

faire une réponse de Normand

> *"to give the reply of a Norman"*
> = not to say yes or no
> = not to give a straight answer

The Normans are proverbial for being cunning and crafty, as are people from Gascony and Le Mans.

Il a fait une réponse de Normand en disant qu'il n'est ni pour ni contre.
He didn't give a straight answer and said he was neither for nor against.

vider son sac *(informal)*

> *"to empty your bag"*
> = to come out with it
> = to get it all off your chest

Vincent, qui d'habitude est plutôt réservé, s'est mis à vider son sac pendant la réunion.
Vincent, who is usually rather reserved, got it all off his chest during the meeting.

avoir voix au chapitre

"to have a voice in the chapter"
= to have a say in the matter
= to have your say

The origin of this expression has nothing to do with chapters in books, but rather with the governing body of a cathedral or monastic order.

C'est un proviseur très moderne qui est persuadé que les lycéens doivent avoir voix au chapitre.
He's a progressive principal who believes that secondary school students ought to have their say.

ménager la chèvre et le chou

"to show consideration for the goat and the cabbage"
= to sit on the fence
= to keep both parties sweet

Try keeping a goat away from a cabbage once it's set eyes on it! In English, *to run with the hare and hunt with the hounds* is equally expressive.

Pour l'instant le gouvernement essaie de ménager la chèvre et le chou, mais bientôt il devra faire un choix.
For the moment the government is trying to keep everybody sweet, but soon it will have to make a decision.

Money, debt, wealth and poverty

tirer le diable par la queue *(informal)*

"*to pull the devil by the tail*"
= to live from hand to mouth

The devil figures in quite a few French idioms.

On devient rarement riche grâce à l'art ; il faut savoir que la plupart des artistes tirent le diable par la queue.
You rarely get rich through art; you have to realize that the majority of artists live from hand to mouth.

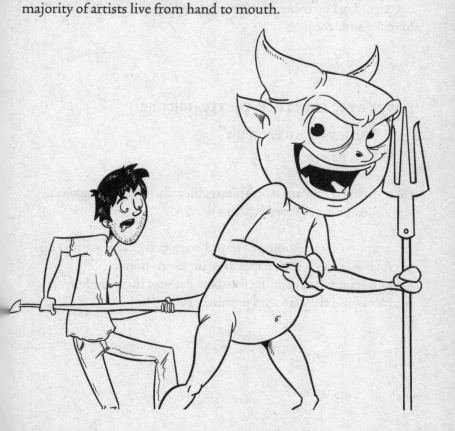

mettre du beurre dans les épinards

> *"to put butter in the spinach"*
> = to help make ends meet

● A staple ingredient in French cooking, butter features in a number of expressions.

Le samedi, je distribue des prospectus : ça ne rapporte pas beaucoup, mais ça met du beurre dans les épinards.
On Saturday I distribute leaflets; it doesn't pay much but it helps to make ends meet.

payer avec un lance-pierre *(informal)*

> *"to pay with a catapult"*
> = to pay peanuts

● manger avec un lance-pierre, literally *to eat with a catapult*, means *to wolf something down*.

Les employés ne restent pas dans l'entreprise car il y a peu de perspectives et ils sont payés avec un lance-pierre.
Employees don't stay in the business because there are few prospects and they are paid peanuts.

coûter les yeux de la tête (informal)

> *"to cost the eyes from the head"*
> = to cost an arm and a leg
> = to cost the earth

Il y a des ordinateurs ultra-perfectionnés qui **coûtent les yeux de la tête**, mais on trouve aussi des modèles abordables.
There are some ultra-sophisticated computers which cost an arm and a leg but you can also find affordable models.

être sur la paille

> *"to be on the straw"*
> = to be penniless

If your bed is made of straw rather than of something more comfortable, then you must be down on your luck.

Quand il a créé son entreprise, François y a mis toutes ses économies. Depuis, l'entreprise a fait faillite et il **est sur la paille**.
When he set up his business, François put all his savings into it. Since then, it has gone bankrupt and he is penniless.

ça ne mange pas de pain

> "it doesn't eat any bread"
>
> = it doesn't cost much

This is one of a number of expressions involving bread.

On peut toujours essayer, ça ne mange pas de pain.
We can always try, it doesn't cost much.

pour une bouchée de pain

> "for a mouthful of bread"
>
> = for a song
>
> = for next to nothing

Les appareils photo qui étaient hors de prix à l'époque se vendent pour une bouchée de pain maintenant.
Cameras which were exorbitant at that time now sell for next to nothing.

coûter bonbon (*informal*)

"*to cost a sweet*"

= to cost an arm and a leg

Ils ont fait installer un jacuzzi dans leur maison ; ça a dû leur coûter bonbon.
They have had a jacuzzi fitted in their house; that must have cost them an arm and a leg.

Language, speech, silence and conversation

clouer le bec à quelqu'un (informal)

"to nail somebody's mouth"

= to reduce somebody to silence

= to shut somebody up

The origin of this expression isn't as brutal as it sounds! **Clouer** is not the modern verb, which means to nail, but the old French word, **clore**, meaning *to shut*.

Quand il a commencé à protester, elle lui a cloué le bec.
When he began to protest she shut him up.

sauter du coq à l'âne

> *"to jump from the cockerel to the donkey"*
> = to jump from one subject to another

⬤ You can also say **passer du coq à l'âne**, literally *to go from the cockerel to the donkey.*

C'est un professeur brillant, mais il n'arrête pas de passer du coq à l'âne et ses cours sont difficiles à suivre.
He's an outstanding teacher but he's forever jumping from one subject to another and his lessons are difficult to follow.

ne pas avoir la langue dans sa poche

> *"not to have your tongue in your pocket"*
> = never to be at a loss for words

⬤ If your tongue isn't hidden away in your pocket, then there is nothing stopping you talking.

Ma petite cousine commence tout juste à parler, mais elle n'a déjà pas la langue dans sa poche.
My little cousin has just started talking but already she is never at a loss for words.

avoir un chat dans la gorge

"to have a cat in your throat"

= to have a frog in your throat

● The French appear to be almost alone on this one; most other European languages opt for the frog or toad.

Le prof avait du mal à parler, il avait un chat dans la gorge.
The teacher had trouble speaking, he had a frog in his throat.

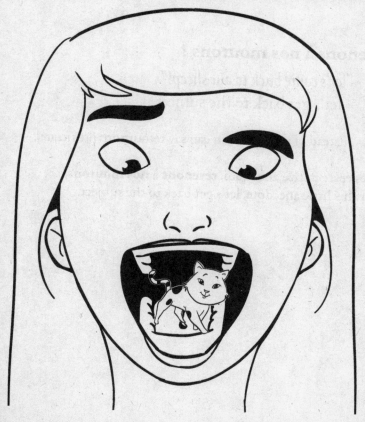

avoir la langue bien pendue

"to have a well-hung tongue"

= to be a gossip

Madame Mercier, notre voisine, a la langue bien pendue ;
quand on fait quelque chose, tout le village est au courant !
Mrs Mercier, our neighbour, is a gossip; when you do something,
the whole village knows about it!

revenons à nos moutons !

"let's come back to our sheep!"

= let's get back to the subject

Instead of **revenons** you can say **retournons** (let's return).

Après cette petite anecdote, revenons à nos moutons.
After this little anecdote, let's get back to the subject.

casser du sucre sur le dos de quelqu'un

> *"to break sugar on somebody's back"*
> = to talk about somebody behind their back

🔵   This expression seems to originate from when sugar was carried around in large blocks rather than the small lumps we are familiar with today.

J'ai du mal à faire confiance à ma collègue Martine : elle a l'air sympa mais elle passe son temps à **casser du sucre sur le dos des autres.**

I find it hard to trust my colleague Martine: she seems friendly but she spends her time talking about other people behind their backs.

parler français comme une vache espagnole
(informal)

> *"to speak French like a Spanish cow"*
> = to absolutely murder the French language

Quand Eamon est arrivé en France il y a trois ans, il **parlait français comme une vache espagnole** ; maintenant il est quasiment bilingue.

When Eamon came to France three years ago he used to absolutely murder the French language; now he is practically bilingual.

être un pince-sans-rire

"to pinch without laughing"
= to have a deadpan sense of humour

Au début, on a l'impression qu'il est froid et triste ; en réalité c'est un pince-sans-rire, on ne s'ennuie jamais avec lui.
At first you think he is cold and rather joyless; in reality he has a deadpan sense of humour, there's never a dull moment with him.

Youth, experience, age and death

passer l'arme à gauche (informal)

"*to pass the weapon to the left*"
= to kick the bucket
= to pop your clogs

One of a number of euphemisms for death, this one is from the military arena. A soldier at ease, i.e. inactive, would have his rifle on the left.

**Après une vie bien remplie,
à quatre-vingt-quinze ans,
il a passé l'arme à gauche.**
After a very full life, at the age
of 95, he popped his clogs.

sentir le sapin (informal)

> *"to smell of fir tree"*
> = to have one foot in the grave

An old French expression alluding to the wood from which coffins were habitually made: if your days are numbered, you'll be starting to notice that pine-fresh smell.

Il tremble de plus en plus : ça sent le sapin.
He's shaking more and more: he's got one foot in the grave.

faire long feu

> *"to make a long fire"*
> = to fizzle out

The idea here is that if the fire in your musket burns too slowly, the musket ball won't go off properly.

Deux ans après la signature du traité, l'alliance entre les deux pays semble avoir fait long feu.
Two years after the signing of the treaty, the alliance between the two countries seems to have fizzled out.

avoir de la bouteille *(informal)*

"to have bottle"

= to have been around a long time

= to be long in the tooth

Wine, of course, is integral to French culture and society – and some wine is kept for a long time. You can also say **prendre de la bouteille** *(to be getting old)*.

Quand j'étais plus jeune, ce genre de problème me contrariait beaucoup, mais plus maintenant : quand on commence à **avoir de la bouteille**, on fait la part des choses.

When I was younger, this kind of problem really annoyed me, but not any more: when you start to get long in the tooth, you make allowances.

manger les pissenlits par la racine *(informal)*

"*to eat dandelions by the root*"
= to be pushing up the daisies
= to be dead and buried

Quand la police a enfin retrouvé sa trace, il mangeait les pissenlits par la racine depuis longtemps.
When the police finally picked up his trail again, he'd already been pushing up the daisies for a long time.

avoir un coup de pompe

"*to be hit by the pump*"
= to feel drained
= to feel shattered

Pour éviter d'avoir un coup de pompe, mangez des sucres lents, des pâtes par exemple.
To avoid feeling drained eat complex sugars, like pasta for example.

casser sa pipe (informal)

"to break your pipe"
= to die
= to buy it

Spanish and German both share this expression, but nobody is sure of its origin.

Je ne sais pas quand je casserai ma pipe ; le plus tard possible, j'espère.
I don't know when I'll buy it; not for a very long time I hope.

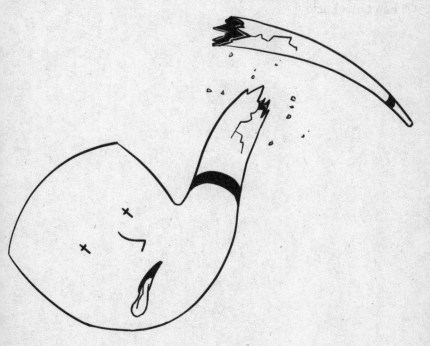

être au bout du rouleau (informal)

"to be at the end of the roll"
= to be exhausted
= to have come to the end of the road

This expression can also be used to talk about running short of money.

À quarante ans à peine, j'avais l'impression d'**être au bout du rouleau. Puis j'ai rencontré Lucie.**
I was only just 40 and I felt I had come to the end of the road. Then I met Lucie.

Index

Easy Learning French Idioms

Have you seen our full French range?
Pick a title to fit your learning style.

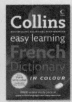

Dictionary
£8.99

Grammar
£6.99

Verbs
£6.99

Collins Easy Learning Series

The bestselling language resources, perfect if you're learning French for the first time or brushing up on rusty skills.

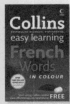

Words
£6.99

Complete 3-in-1
volume
£10.99

Conversation
£6.99

Collins Easy Learning Audio Courses

This exciting course allows learners to absorb the basics at home or on the move, without the need for thick textbooks and complex grammar.

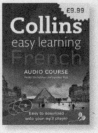